Advance Praise for *Untenable*

"A startlingly honest and poignant look at 'white flight' from the white perspective. A necessary and overdue corrective."

— **Brent Bozell III**, founder and president
of the Media Research Center

Also by Jack Cashill

The Hunt
Unmasking Obama: The Fight to Tell the
True Story of a Failed Presidency
Barack Obama's Promised Land: Deplorables Need Not Apply

Untenable

The *True* Story of White Ethnic
Flight from America's Cities

JACK CASHILL

Post Hill
PRESS

A POST HILL PRESS BOOK
ISBN: 978-1-63758-646-4
ISBN (eBook): 978-1-63758-647-1

Untenable:
The True Story of White Ethnic Flight from America's Cities
© 2023 by Jack Cashill
All Rights Reserved

Cover design by Joel Gilbert

This is a work of nonfiction. All people, locations, events, and situation are portrayed to the best of the author's memory.

Post Hill Press
New York • Nashville
posthillpress.com

Published in the United States of America
1 2 3 4 5 6 7 8 9 10

Dedicated to Newark Police Detective William F. Cashill

TABLE OF CONTENTS

SNOW FALLS ON PIGS

The call came to my house in Kansas City on December 15, 1981. I remember the date well. It was my birthday. That night my wife, Joan, and I had tickets to see the Rolling Stones. We thought we might not get the chance again. After all, Mick Jagger was nearing forty.

I did not expect the call. The employer in question had turned me down months earlier for "political" reasons. Complicating matters, I had another offer pending, this one in Berkeley. I had good friends who lived there. They lobbied hard for their once charmed city. The restaurants are fabulous, they told me, so, too, the wineries, the scenery, and, of course, the weather. They were disappointed when I told them I wasn't coming. They were shocked when I told them where I was going.

"Newark," I said, rhyming it with "pork" as God intended.

"As in New Jersey?"

"The one and the same."

"But why?"

"Simple," I said. "It's home."

cʒ

At its purest, home was a night like that of March 19, 1958, when snow, loads of it, all the more welcome for its late arrival, fell on Pigs. Pigs was shorthand for Pigtails Alley, the magical stretch of broken asphalt and ground glass that ran unseen by adult eyes down the length of our block before doglegging to the west just short of block's end.

With the snow falling so abundantly, no one needed prompting. We all came out. From the Myrtle Avenue side, it was me and my brother Bob, Irish twins, born within a year of each other, he the older, a fact he never let me forget. From down Myrtle a few houses came broken-home Bobby. From the Roseville Avenue side, directly across Pigs, came Richie, our leader, and his wild little brother Ronnie. From farther down Roseville were Roger and his pesky little brother Norman, Sean and his wee little brother Brendan, and Earl, my fellow Dodger fan. From Orange Street, the commercial corridor at block's end, came Bobby and his older, slightly "touched" brother George, and Artie, a little scrapper we had captured not long before. From farther up Roseville came Paul, the rarest of all local fauna, an only child, and Donato, new not just to the block but to the country.

In a way, we were all new to the country. Nearly every one of us had living relatives who had been born elsewhere—Ireland, Italy, Germany, Hungary. Earl was the exception. His family had been in America since at least 1808, the year the Constitution banned the importation of slaves. We were "diverse" then without knowing or caring that we were. According to the 1950 census, immigrants from fourteen different countries, including outliers like Finland and Turkey, lived on just the Myrtle side of the block.

In Pigs, none of that mattered. All that did matter was if you could run fast enough and dive hard enough on your Flexible Flyer to sled headfirst down to the dogleg. The slope in Pigs was lively enough to keep us flying all night. With the alley's sole streetlight already lit, we had no natural signal to call the evening over. We did have, however, my father, a police officer and the most authoritative presence on the block. At some point, he would sense the time was right for his signature whistle, a beckoning homeward as final and plaintive as "Taps"—a long low note, a short high note, a long low note. Upon hearing it, we all knew the sledding was done and God was nigh.

That wintry night in March, the snow was general all over the northeast. Kids like us in cities big and small, from Camden to Chicago, from Buffalo to Baltimore, were out sledding on their slopes, many likely steeper than ours, but none as special. In Pigs, as elsewhere, we knew these moments would not last forever, but we had no idea how short-lived they would be. Within a dozen years, give or take, our families, thousands of them, hundreds of thousands, millions, would be coldly uprooted and randomly dispersed.

In our case, the removal would be swift and brutal. By the end of the 1960s, the state had razed many of our homes, mine included. A lethal riot had scorched the neighborhood. My friends and their families had scattered to the winds, and a twenty-foot-deep trench as wide as a tennis court forever severed the north end of Pigs from the south. To the degree anyone beyond our world noticed, it was to scold us for our very displacement.

Within five years of that snowy March night, some of the same forces that scattered us led to the sudden and shocking death of my father, a gentleman from sole to crown. It is for his sake, and the sake of all the dispossessed, that I share the saga of our unwelcome diaspora. "Tell the story of your village," said Dostoevsky. "If you tell it well, you will have told the story of the world."[1]

UNTENABLE

In her massive 2018 bestseller, *Becoming*, and on the arena tour that followed, Michelle Obama laid out for the world her version of "White flight." Michelle was at her harshest and most specific at a 2019 Obama Foundation forum. "As families like ours, upstanding families like ours, who were doing everything we were supposed to do and better, as we moved in, White folks moved out," she told the moderator, adding, "They were afraid of what our families represented."

To drive the injustice home, Michelle, pointing to herself and to her mild-mannered brother Craig, continued, "I wanna remind White folks that y'all were running from us, and y'all still runnin'." Among the things that unnerved White people, said Michelle, were "the color of our skin" and the "texture of our hair."[2]

My friends from Pigs have a slightly different take on White flight. I asked one lifelong friend, a loyal Democrat, why he and his widowed mother finally left our block in the early 1970s, twenty years after the first African American families moved in. He searched a minute for the right set of words and then simply said, "It became untenable." When I asked what "untenable" meant," he answered, "When your mother gets mugged for the *second* time, that's untenable. When your home gets broken into for the *second* time, that's untenable."

There is no understanding what really happened to Newark and other troubled cities without knowing a little about the White ethnics who inhabited those cities and their attachment to the neighborhoods they lived in. Almost to a person, they or their kin came to America for the very qualities now sadly absent in too many cities: freedom, security, the rule of law, opportunity. For the first Cashill to come to America, that opportunity was a lifeline.

Not until I came back to Newark in 1982 did I discover who that first Cashill was. With little to guide me, I stumbled upon his grave on a spooky summer eve in St. Paul's Cemetery on Nassau Street in Princeton. After much wandering about, I found my great-great-grandfather, John Cashell, from County Waterford in Ireland. His American-born son, John D. Cashill, was buried nearby. So, too, was John D.'s wife, Catherine Kane Cashill, and her father—an unexpected find—great-great-granddad Patrick Kane from County Cavan.

Names changed frequently in those days. The original John Cashell's descendants went by either "Cashill" or "Cashel," but not "Cashell," the name on the elder John's tombstone. As a brief aside, while still in academia, I attended a presentation by two Rutgers professors who had an insight on name changes. The two made a film starring themselves canoeing up New Jersey's Raritan River and embarking at Ellis Island. There they inflicted on each other the kind of indignities they imagined the new arrivals suffered, none more heartrending than the butchering of the newcomers' names. So traumatic was the experience that the profs thought it fair to compare Ellis Island to—hang on here—Auschwitz. During the Q & A, I suggested that since the average immigrant spent only an hour or two on Ellis Island, might not the local DMV be a more apt point of comparison than a Nazi crematorium? As the reader might suspect, I was not long for academe.

John and his wife, Ann, set out from Waterford for America in 1847—Black '47, as the Irish call it—the darkest year of that country's horrific potato famine. Reading about the famine makes one realize how relative, when used in a contemporary American context, are words like "poverty," "hunger," or "hard times." The blight hit the potato-rich County Waterford particularly hard. A local reporter shared his observations: "The poor are dying like rotten sheep, in fact they are melting down into the clay by the sides of the ditches.... The bodies remain for whole weeks in those places unburied. In a corner of the vegetable shambles, a man was dead for five days."[3] In a word, Ireland had become untenable.

Those who could get out got out. Those who could not, many of them at least, died—more than a million dead and another million departed during the four famine years, 1845–49. Another million would leave in the next decade, nearly halving the country's population. John's landlord in Ireland, either out of charity or greed, may have paid his passage to America. This happened often. Whatever his motive, the landlord could then rededicate the vacated property to more productive purposes than, say, growing rotten potatoes. It is possible, too, that John and Ann had their passage paid by an American farmer in exchange for a period of indentured servitude. That happened as well. In any case, John first shows up on the census as a laborer living in rural New Jersey.

I do not know the details of John and Ann's departure, but an estimated 20 percent of those who left Ireland for North America in 1847 did not reach our shores alive. There were many ways to die en route, none of them pretty. John and Ann were among the blessed. By extension, so too was I. Their exodus enabled me to come of age in the most bountiful nation in the most bountiful time in the history of the world. The Irish are legendary for their grudges, but I have not earned the right to bear one against whoever sent John and Ann packing.

If "poverty" can only be understood as a relative term in an American context, the same holds true for "diaspora," a word derived from the Greek for "disperse." In the nineteenth century, when Irish emigrants approached their departure date, friends and family would stage an "American wake," less in their honor than in their memory. These were melancholy affairs. The folks left behind did not expect to see the departed ever again. By contrast, when ethnic neighborhoods emptied in America, those leaving had at least the hope of maintaining contact with their old friends and neighbors, even if they rarely did.

The one burden we had to bear that our ancestors did not was the contempt of our betters for "fleeing." Here is how Robin DiAngelo, among the most influential "antiracists," sums up our collective plight: "White families fled from cities to the suburbs to escape the influx of people of color, a process socialogists [*sic*] term White flight. They wrote covenants to keep schools and neighborhoods segregated and forbade cross-racial dating."[4] DiAngelo's analysis of "White flight" is no more accurate than her spelling of "sociologist." Nonetheless, she makes more than $700,000 a year reminding smug White people of the "fragility" of their less enlightened peers. Were DiAngelo—born Robin Taylor—to tell the true story of America's Great Ethnic Diaspora, her speaking fees would shrivel to nothing.

Unlike DiAngelo, Amiri Baraka expressed at least an interest in the fate of the displaced. Born Leroy Jones, later changed to LeRoi Jones, Baraka grew up in an integrated neighborhood less than a mile from where I did and attended our local high school, Barringer. After speaking of his White acquaintances, Baraka writes in his useful memoir, *The Autobiography of LeRoi Jones*, "I often wonder what those guys and girls carried away from that experience with us and what they make of it."[5] Unfortunately, Baraka never got around to asking. Then again, if he had asked, and had listened, he might never have been named New Jersey poet laureate. He got that title by neither knowing nor caring.

It is remarkable, given the social and political consequences of their exodus, that no one of note has asked "those guys and girls" what they made of their experience in America's collapsing cities. If writers had asked, they would have learned quickly just how fruitless it is to find meaning in the collective "whiteness" of the urban dispossessed. In Newark, as elsewhere, each ethnic group reacted differently to the pressures brought to bear on its neighborhood. Of course, too, White ethnics were not the only ones to "flee." Blacks, Hispanics, and Asians left the cities for much the same reasons urban

Whites did, but only Whites were shamed for leaving, thus the word "White" in the book's title.

In February 2009, weeks after Barack Obama's inauguration, Attorney General Eric Holder caught heat for saying what is obviously true: "Though this nation has proudly thought of itself as an ethnic melting pot, in things racial we have always been and continue to be, in too many ways, essentially a nation of cowards." Holder elaborated, again accurately, "Certain subjects are off limits and that to explore them risks at best embarrassment and at worst the questioning of one's character." Unfortunately, Holder's observation is more true now than then—in no small part due to the ready use of racial slander by Holder and his allies. Given the precarious racial zeitgeist, I will use just the first names of those who spoke with me about our shared experience. As to my childhood friends, I will use the names I knew you by then. Sorry, guys.

This shared experience enables me to write with some confidence about Newark in general and "White flight" writ large. About the collapse of Roseville, my own neighborhood, it enables me to write authoritatively. We were there. We saw it. We know what we saw. In 1975, *Time* magazine would call Newark "the worst city in America." Those of us who lived there know why. Our city suffered every form of governmental abuse, local and national, a modern democracy can dish out. Newark's shellacking was extreme but not exceptional. A half-dozen other New Jersey cities—and scores more throughout the Northeast and Midwest—suffered similar abuse.

As the Department of Justice reminds us, it is important to know the impact—"emotional, physical, and financial"—a crime has had on its victims.[6] Consider what follows a victim impact statement. Those eager to "blame the victim" are reading the wrong book.

WORKING GIRLS

Given that no adult ever visited Pigtails Alley—save for the occasional rummy—the alley's original purpose was lost to history. When I posted a photo of Pigs on a neighborhood Facebook page, a local real estate reporter asked about the name. Richie, from across the alley, posted, "The story is that years and years ago they raised pigs in that area, that's the only story I ever heard."

I chimed in, "That is basically the same story I heard."

Other than in my own postings, "Pigtails Alley" shows up absolutely nowhere on Google. Neighborhood history, however, suggests a rationale for the alley's name and function. Until about 1850, the area had been farmland. The first street opened was Myrtle Avenue, just a block long. Roseville Avenue was likely the second north-south street. Orange Street meanwhile was emerging as the dominant east-west commercial corridor. If a farmer wanted to bring his pigs to market on Orange Street, local developers would not want him to drive those noisome little porkers down their newly platted streets. Just as Pigs sheltered us kids from querulous neighbors, Pigs likely did much the same for the pigs. The dogleg on to Myrtle would allow the farmer to muster his charges before releasing them into the traffic on Orange. Or so I imagine.

The name for the area was almost as elusive as the name for the alley at its center. There are competing theories, but the best guess is that the neighborhood took the name "Roseville" from James Rowe, a popular landowner. His granddaughter certainly thought so. She would later claim, "In his modesty, Rowe requested that the letter 'W' be deleted from the community's name for a more picturesque title."[7]

Whatever the source of the name, Roseville was changing. Not everyone was happy about the changes. Miss Elizabeth Bathgate, whose family had a local street named in its honor, wrote in longhand a cranky history of the neighborhood now preserved by the Newark Public Library. Bathgate saw an area "marked by transition from the age-old farms-sustaining way of life to the age of industrial life." Stabilizing the neighborhood, from her perspective, were three establishment churches: Presbyterian, Methodist, and Episcopal. Together, they "had made united effort to hold a standard of living where character was the primary consideration. That standard was threatened by the new era coming to birth."[8]

That new era prompted the opening of the one church that would soon emerge as the real standard-bearer of the neighborhood, St. Rose of Lima. "I thought," said founding father, Fr. McKeever, "that there was a singular appropriateness in having a St. Rose in Roseville."[9] When the first mass was served in 1888 above the Roseville skating rink, there were only twenty-seven identified Catholics in the vicinity. By the time I started school at St. Rose, one would have had to look hard to find twenty-seven non-Catholics.

The growth of Roseville mirrored the growth of Newark, much as the growth of Newark mirrored that of most industrial cities in the northeast and the north-central United States. British or Dutch founding fathers yield their farmlands to developers. The developers attract entrepreneurs and industrialists. And families from all over the world smell opportunity in the transition.

The Cashill family evolved much as Newark did. John Cashell would prove to be the family's last farmhand. His son, John D. Cashill, found work as a tinsmith in Princeton. If proof were needed of the family's swift Americanization, John D. provided it by naming his seventh and last child William Jennings Bryan Cashill. "Willie" entered the world kicking in May 1897, seven months after his namesake's crucifixion on "a cross of gold" in the 1896 presidential election. By 1900, for reasons that surely made more sense then than now, John moved his growing brood from Princeton to Newark.

My family history was unexceptional for baby boom urban Americans, especially those in Newark. Of my eight great-grandparents, five had been born abroad. Six of the eight had their roots in Ireland, two in Germany. By 1900, all of them had found their way to an American city, seven of them to New Jersey. "The city of Newark is undergoing the most astonishing changes," said Newark Mayor Henry Doremus in 1907. Some 250,000 immigrants had arrived in the city just in the years between 1870 and 1910. They swelled Newark's population from 136,500 in 1880 to 347,000 in 1910. "It is to be doubted," said a city historian in 1913, "if more than a few hundred who can trace their lineage back to the founders still remain in Newark."[10]

Three of my grandparents grew up in families with a half dozen or more children. The fourth was one of three. The privileges they enjoyed as White Americans did not include electricity or indoor plumbing. In that era, cities literally stank of shite, human and horse, the former flowing through the gutters after a rain, the latter piling up in the streets regardless of the weather. Cholera came in waves. Tuberculosis haunted even the more affluent households. Willie's mom died before he was ten. That was not unusual. The average life span for an American woman in that era was forty-eight. Catherine Kane Cashill made it to forty-nine. Still, for all their travails, these were among the healthiest and best-fed city dwellers in the world.

The word "teenager" had yet to enter the lexicon. Urban kids typically went to work as soon as they were old enough to help support their families. In his fair-minded book, *Children of the City*, David Nasaw explores the multitudinous ways in which enterprising youngsters chipped in to keep their struggling families afloat, girls even more than boys. "The loyalty and sacrifice of teenage girls to their families was legendary,"[11] writes Nasaw. Life was tough for these children of immigrants, but by and large, it was not nearly as tough as it had been for their parents or those still laboring at the kind of jobs their ancestors fled. "Compared to their rural counterparts locked inside mines, mills, and canneries or put out to work on sugar beet, cotton, and berry fields," writes Nasaw, "they were privileged."[12] In America, their ultimate privilege was the privilege of possibility. It did not come in a color.

Bernard Berg, a Jewish immigrant from Ukraine, believed in that possibility. In the first decade of the twentieth century he opened up a pharmacy at 36 South 13th Street, a five-minute walk from my future home on Myrtle Avenue. He and his wife, Rose, and their three children lived upstairs from the store where Bernard worked fifteen hours a day. "They were old world people from the other side who seemed grateful to be here," an Irish neighbor remembered. "They were trying to be Americans, to blend right in. They weren't greedy."[13]

The Jews in Roseville had to deal with stereotypes, "greedy" being one, but on the whole they were well received. Rose Katz and her family were the only Jews on her block. Her neighbors "would occasionally start with the now well-known remark 'you are different from other Jews,'" Rose remembers. "Then I would explain that I am not different and that they were merely misinformed about the Jewish people. That is how we became very good neighbors indeed."[14]

If being ambitious for one's children was a stereotype, Bernard would have to plead guilty. Unlike most neighborhood kids, the Berg children didn't work. They studied. In time, the studying paid off. The oldest child, Samuel, graduated from med school and returned to the neighborhood to practice medicine. Well respected as a physician, he was better remembered as a photographer. Between the years 1959 and 1968, the then sixty-something Samuel decided to photograph Newark with a particular emphasis on Roseville. The Berg Picture Collection at the Newark Public Library contains twenty-seven hundred of his photos. The second child, Ethel, rose to prominence as an educator, and she, too, remained in Roseville. The third child, Morris, deserves his own book. In fact, several books have been written and a movie or two have been made, but more about Morris "Moe" Berg later.

The young women of Roseville got a seeming break in 1917 when a new business opened in the neighborhood. The founders of the Radium Luminous Material Corporation chose Newark in no small part because of the growing pool of immigrant children ready to work. Offering a job that was relatively easy and borderline glamorous, they had no shortage of applicants.

My German grandmother, Marie Mueller, then sixteen, was living nearby with her parents and her seven brothers and sisters. She could have been one of the new hires had she not married Willie Cashill the same year the company opened its doors. If this mixed marriage made waves at the time, the shock of it did not register in family lore. In Newark it is hard to find an Irishman without a German somewhere in the woodpile.

With World War I looming, the tall, blue-eyed Willie, now twenty, found work at the Hercules Powder Company in Parlin, New Jersey. He took the job knowing of the dangers. Katherine Schaub, who lived just a few blocks from Marie in Newark, started her new job at the radium "studio" with no such apprehension.

A year younger than Marie and also the daughter of German immigrants, Katherine shared a dwelling with seven members of her extended family, among them her orphaned cousin Irene Rudolph. Soon to be fifteen, Katherine had graduated from elementary school, education enough for an immigrant child of either sex in that era. On February 1, 1917, Katherine walked the four blocks to the studio on Third Street excited to get to work. The new company was the talk of the neighborhood.

"A friend of mine told me about the 'watch studio' where watch-dial numerals and hands were painted with a luminous substance that made them visible in the dark," Katherine would later recount. "The work, she explained, was interesting and of a far higher type than the usual factory job."[15] Her supervisor Anna Rooney, not quite thirty at the time and of Irish stock, lived just a block from the studio. She showed the pretty young blonde how the job was done.

To keep the paint brushes moist, the women would wet the tips with their lips. When Katherine broke out in pimples she was concerned enough to consult a doctor. He threw a scare into Katherine, suggesting that her job may have caused the acne. Alarmed, she took her concerns to her supervisors. They assured Katherine and the other women that the radium was safe in the small doses to which they were exposed. Management knew no more than the women did. Nor did Madam Curie for that matter. She would die from exposure to radium. Industrial America was learning on the job.

After a year at the studio, Katherine was pleased to find a position for her cousin Irene. The business was booming. In 1920, management moved the growing company a few miles west to Orange. Irene and Katherine stuck with it. Even before the move, however, Katherine had begun to notice a "cracking and stiffness of her legs." Irene meanwhile began to experience infections and inflammations in her mouth that baffled the doctors who treated her. "The decay in Irene's jaw was eating her alive," writes Kate Moore in her well-deserved bestseller, *The Radium Girls*, "bit by bit." Not until 1923 did a doctor suspect radium to be the source of the girls' ailments, and even then few of his peers believed him. In July 1923, Irene, just twenty-one, died in agony. Despite entreaties from many of the dying women and their families, the New Jersey Department of Labor took no action.

Katherine lived longer than her cousin and, if possible, suffered even more. An activist and aspiring writer, Katherine took her case to the county medical examiner who finally confirmed radium as the culprit. For those already poisoned, there was to be no cure. "The county medical examiner's diagnosis," wrote Katherine, "furnished perfect legal evidence for a lawsuit." The lawsuit launched by Katherine and her co-workers captured the attention of the nation, and that attention persuaded their employer to settle on terms favorable to the women. The money, however, could not reverse radium's demonic course. Katherine lingered longer than she would have liked and died a gruesome death at thirty.

The wheels of justice ground slowly for the "radium girls," but they did grind. Unlike in Germany or in Ireland or in the Jim Crow South, citizens of Newark expected equal justice under the law. They didn't always get it, but collectively they got it often enough that they never lost that expectation.

ETHNIC CLEANSING

By 1920, Willie and Marie Cashill had found their way back to Newark, along with son Billy, my father, who turned two that May. The census of that year listed Willie's occupation as "sheet metal worker." He and his family were living at 354 Bremen Street, an address I was unable to find on a contemporary map. From what I could tell, this was a heavily German neighborhood. My suspicions as to why I could not find it on the map were confirmed with a little more research.

Not unlike the anti-Russian sentiment stoked by the media in 2022 over the Ukrainian invasion, outrage over Germany's conduct in World War I, real and imagined, swept America, Newark included. After the US entered the war in 1917, German Americans were wise to keep their heads down. Although my great-grandfather retained the name Mueller, more than a few Muellers became Millers, and product names changed as well. Frankfurters were already known as "hot dogs," and no one messed with "hamburger," but sauerkraut endured the temporary indignity of being called "liberty cabbage."

In 1918, Newark did its own little bit to feed the anti-German frenzy by changing the name of eight of its streets.

The Board of Commissioners voted unanimously to purge from the collective memory Bismarck Avenue, Dresden Street, Berlin Street, German Street, Frankfort Street, Frederick Street, Hamburg Place, and, yes, Bremen Street. Bremen Street was renamed "Marne Street" after the 1914 battle that reversed the early tide of the war. Despite the mania, city hall moved as sluggishly then as now. In 1920, census takers still listed my grandparents' address as "Bremen Street." On a side note, Berlin Street became "Rome Street." This change recognized the contributions to the war effort of Italy, our then ally.[16] A century later, Newark Italians would watch in disgust as city hall coldly erased their own heritage.

Quick to assimilate, German Americans stepped up the process during and after World War I. Despite the language obstacle, they blended well and quickly. By my era, I knew of no German neighborhood, told no German jokes, and had no useful anti-German slur beyond "Hotsy-Totsy another Nazi." Italians, Blacks, Poles, and even the Irish remained fair game, but not the Germans. Despite their numbers, they assimilated so fully they seem to have disappeared. World War II, I suspect, hastened the disappearance.

Speaking of disappearances, I return to the story of Willie, Marie, and little Billy. To tell their story in full, I will jump forward to 1960. In August of that year, my parents, my brother Bob, my sister Maureen, and I drove from New Jersey to Florida to visit Nana and Gramps. I had met them only once before in 1952, but at four, I recalled little of that trip. One thing that I do remember is stopping to pick up my mother's immigrant grandmother to ride with us. At the time, Grandma Belleville, as we called her, was eighty-six years old. She rode in the back seat with me and my five-year-old brother for three pre-interstate, pre-air-conditioned days. Bless her hardy little heart! I regret never having thought to ask why she came along for the ride.

In 1960, divided highways took us no farther than Maryland. From there, it was US Highway 301 all the way to Madeira Beach, near St. Petersburg, where Nana and Gramps lived. Toward the end of each day's drive, we started looking hard for a motel that offered two essentials—air-conditioning and a swimming pool. Many offered neither. We needed both. Our 1950 Buick had, of course, no air-conditioning, no seat belts for that matter. We somehow survived their absence.

At the time, 301 ran through and around the towns of the Jim Crow South inland from the coast. Other than the Burma-Shave signs, what struck me as most distinctive about the South were the separate bathrooms for Blacks and Whites. Not having seen these in New Jersey, I asked my father for his take on the phenomenon. Always more of a pragmatist than a moralist, he told me they made no sense as they cost the taxpayers twice as much to install.

That said, my father instinctively did what was right. At a rest stop, on a Sunday morning, we encountered a Black couple dressed for church. For some reason, I remember vividly the white, frilly dress that their little girl wore. The parents looked distressed. When my father inquired, the dad explained that the car had died on the way to church. Always handy, Dad pulled out the jumper cables and offered to help. The other dad seemed surprised by the offer but was hugely grateful for the assistance. Apparently, the family had been stuck there for quite some time. The mom commented favorably on our license plates. As their car roared to life, I felt proud of my father and prouder still to be from New Jersey.

Later on a side trip to Miami, our car sputtered to a halt on the Tamiami Trail, then a lonely, two-lane road through the Everglades. My father quickly diagnosed the problem as a broken fan belt and started hitching a ride back to the nearest town. Soon, a pickup truck stopped with a Seminole Indian at the wheel. He offered my father a ride, and Dad jumped in without hesitation. About two hours later, Dad came back with a fan belt. Visibly relieved, my mother had envisioned the Seminole robbing my father and feeding him to the alligators. I had more confidence in the fellow than that. As kids, we grew up thinking Indians were cool. Dad replaced the broken fan belt without sweat, and we were on our way.

Florida I mostly remember as being hot outdoors and nearly as hot in. Nana, however, seemed indifferent to the heat. Heat was a constant. She could adapt to that. Harder to accept was the deterioration of her body. Chronic arthritis had twisted her hands—though not so much she couldn't hold a cigarette—and so weakened her legs that she was unable to walk. Not yet sixty, she had been confined to a wheelchair for at least twenty years. Gramps made her life worth living. Wiry but strong, he would often just pick Nana up and carry her wherever she needed to go.

In the grandfather department, central casting could not have done better than Gramps. He did all the things TV grandfathers did and then some. He carved faces out of coconuts and put ships in bottles. He took Bob and me fishing and suffered our whining without complaint. Cooler still, from our perspective anyhow, were the missing fingers from his days as a carpenter. Their absence added to his authenticity, as did his bald, bronzed head and the ropy veins in his arms.

Only late in our weeklong stay did I notice something amiss—my father called Gramps "Bernie." Even at twelve, that caught my attention. When I asked my father why he called his dad "Bernie," he sighed, "Long story." Later, when he had Bob and me alone, he told us as much as he thought we could handle. An older cousin of my father's added detail just a few years ago when I caught up with her in St. Petersburg.

Willie apparently was something of a rounder. He drank and gambled, two vices easily satisfied in 1920s Newark, though at the time neither was legal. These habits may well have put him in debt to some unsavory gentlemen. In Newark, there were quite a few people who fit that description, at least the unsavory part. Chief among them in our world were Richie "the Boot" Boiardo and later his son, "Tony Boy" Boiardo. David Chase, the creator of HBO's *The Sopranos*, has identified the Boiardos as the models for Newark's most prominent fictional family.

The senior Boiardo was born in Naples seven years before Willie Cashill was born in Princeton. By the late 1920s, thanks in large part to Prohibition, Boiardo was nearing the peak of his lethal powers. Boiardo and his crew operated out of Newark's heavily Italian First Ward, which was separated from Roseville by the long, linear, and surprisingly agreeable Branch Brook Park.

My cousin told me that Willie Cashill, when last spoken to, said he had to go meet some guys in Branch Brook Park. He was never seen or heard from again, not a word. Ever. As I later learned, Branch Brook was Boiardo territory. One detail in Richard Linnett's compelling book on the Boiardos, *In the Godfather Garden: The Long Life and Times of Richie "the Boot" Boiardo*, caught my attention. Linnett spoke of a Boiardo enforcer, Ronald Castellano, "who lured a loan-shark victim to Branch Brook in Newark and stabbed him in the stomach."[17] I suspect luring victims to the relative wilds of Branch Brook Park was something of a practice for the Boiardo crew. If so, Willie may have ended his life on the business end of a creditor's knife.

The date of Willie's disappearance is uncertain. He was listed in a 1927 city directory as a "driver," but by the time of the 1930 census, he was gone. Marie and Billy were living with Marie's mother, Mathilde Mueller, back in Roseville in the apartment where Marie grew up. Living there too was a "roomer" from Norway named Bernhard Sorboe.

Years later, after posting the family history on my website, at least as well as I knew it, I received an email from a woman named Toril wanting to know more about Gramps. "I stumbled upon your website yesterday searching for a near relative, Bernhard Sorboe," she wrote. "I already knew that in 1930 he lived in Newark as a roomer in the household of Marie Cashill, and I have found his death certificate in Pinella [*sic*], Florida in 1961. I find it so exciting that I might have found someone who perhaps could tell me some more of his life in the United States."

In response, I gave her the whole spiel about Bernie—saintly guy, totally dependable, took care of my grandmother, the works. "He was the perfect grandfatherly type," I elaborated. "I remember him as being crusty and wiry and funny. He was missing a few fingers from his carpentry days, which impressed us enormously." Below is what she emailed back to me:

> Hi, Jack, Thank you so much for answering me, this is a very strange moment for my husband, Sten and his family.
>
> I have a very strange and also sad story to tell you, hope you are sitting down? First of all, Bernhard Sorboe was Norwegian, not German (as stated on your homepage), and the Norwegian way of writing his name is Bernhard Johann Sørbøe.
>
> Bernhard was born in Bergen, Norway January 5th 1892. His mother died in childbirth when he was 4 years old. His father remarried the following year and the family moved to Kragerø, a small town on the south coast of Norway. I don't believe Bernhard had a happy childhood. At the age of appr. 22 Bernhard married Anna Pauline Jørgensen and they had 7 children, born between 1915 and 1924. Bernhard was a fisherman (owned 3 fishing boats) and a carpenter. I am enclosing the only picture we have of him as a young man.

As in the USA, there were hard times in the end of the 1920's in Norway. Bernhard went to New York to work on a building project. The family story is that he was on his way home, when the ship sunk and he, and everyone else on the ship, drowned. We will never know if his wife knew the truth (she died in 1943), but all of his children grew up believing he was dead.

I became interested in genealogy about 10 years ago, and after a while I thought it would be nice to find out more about the ship that sunk. I can't tell you how surprised we were when I found Bernhard in the 1930 census. Still we weren't sure it was the same man, until a cousin of Sten obtained his death certificate.

Nobody knew that he continued to live in the USA, and the reactions have varied when being told. His two youngest daughters are still alive, but they refuse to accept the truth. A couple of his grandchildren told us they were hurt, they could have needed a grandfather growing up. But most of them found it strange and somewhat exciting. We will probably never know why he acted as he did.

Bernhard has a large family living in Norway, 2 daughters, about 20 grandchildren and numerous great grandchildren. His youngest half-sister is still living, she will be 101 years old in December. My husband is one of Bernhard's grandchildren.

Sten was thrilled to read your letter, and we would like to have as much information (and pictures) as possible. It means a lot to hear from someone who has actually met him. We have learned that two of Bernhard's half-sisters visited him in New York (must have been just before or around the time he went missing) and they told their children, that he was in a bad state. We are so pleased that he seemed to have recovered and lived a good life.

Looking forward to hearing from you again, Toril

Bernhard Sorboe spent the last thirty years of his life taking care of my grandmother, who, as I would later learn, was not the world's easiest woman to take care of. I have to think it was his way of atoning for his own sins. I wondered on occasion whether my grandfather, if he survived his Branch Brook rendezvous, ever got the same chance.

GEORGIA TECH

Not only were the times tougher during the Great Depression, but the cold was colder, the hot hotter, the wind windier, the snow deeper, the rain wetter, and the distances farther than they have been before or since. No child in baby boom America failed to hear some variation on this story: their parents walking miles to school through multiple feet of snow with temperatures many degrees below zero. Some of the storytelling was fanciful, of course, but much of it was not. To understand the response of our parents to the death of their communities, it helps to know what they endured to bring those communities to life.

As a kid, my father's timing could not have been much worse. His father abandoned him when he was about ten. Left with his crippled mother and cranky German grandmother— the only German he learned was the phrase for "shut the door"—Bill got to experience depression living before the Great Depression even started. Although he never lamented his fate, we sensed the trials of his early life through the lessons he tried to teach us.

If we asked him, for instance, to buy a kite, he would sit up startled and say unbelievingly, "Buy? You want to *buy* a *kite?*" He would then show us how to make one out of old newspapers and basket staves. "Staves" was a new word for us. But no Depression story topped the football story. "Football?" Dad told us that at our age he would take a number 10 can and wrap it in old newspapers. Voila, a football! We didn't even know what a number 10 can was.

In 1932, the worst year of the Depression, Bill graduated from grade school. Given the lack of jobs available, he continued on to high school, Newark Central, Junior Soprano's alma mater, vo-tech option. At about thirteen or so, I came across Dad's high school yearbook. To my surprise, I found him, in uniform, pictured with the Central High football team. When I asked why he never talked about playing, he answered, "I never did play." On Saturday, game day, "Big Bill"—all six feet, two hundred pounds of him—had to work. Sadder still was the listing under his photo of "college." Even at thirteen, I knew I had a better chance of being the first teen selected for a NASA mission than he did of going to "Georgia Tech." Those trying times thwarted thousands of dreams.

The arrival of my mother's family in Roseville paralleled that of my father's. Fran Purcell's great-grandfather Patrick Purcell, then thirty, came to America from Ireland in 1860. Patrick's wife, Bridget Giblin, arrived in 1854. The couple had eight children, the youngest of whom, Andrew, was born in 1871. The 1900 census found Andrew living in Providence in the boarding house of the English-born Mary Murphy McGrath. This widowed mother of two was five years older than Andrew. A book could be written about the role of "boarders" and "roomers" in American history. In any case,

Andrew and Mary married in August 1900, and their son, Andy Purcell, my grandfather, was born a year later.

Fran's maternal grandparents, Michael Waters and Mary Clifford Waters, arrived in 1886 and 1888 respectively, the last of my great-grandparents to reach these fair shores. They had eight children; the first six were girls, the last two boys, all of them born poorer than dirt in Jersey City. My grandmother Loretta was the sixth of the six girls. Like my great-grandmother Catherine Cashill, Mary Waters died before she turned fifty. Michael lived a hard seventy-six years. In 1920, he was working as a grinder at a fertilizer plant, arguably the least glamorous job in our unglamorous state.

In 1921, my eighteen-year-old grandmother Loretta Waters married the more worldly nineteen-year-old Andy Purcell. My mother, Frances, was born in 1923 and her brother Bob in 1928. By 1930, Andy was working as a truck driver, Loretta as a waitress. The family had settled into Roseville in a six-unit apartment building above a storefront on busy Orange Street. This mixed-ethnic neighborhood skewed German. There were few Italians thereabout, but my grandfather did not allow my mother to play with those who were there. I have to wonder whether, in years past, the Germans forbade their kids from playing with the Irish.

My father's 1936 Central High School yearbook held an additional surprise, one that I discovered only recently. Inscribed on my father's individual photo were the words, "All my love, Fran." I did a double take on this one. Fran, my mother, did not graduate from *grade* school at St. Rose's until 1937. Taking another look, I saw that Fran had dated her signature "1937." I had to question whether she backdated it to keep my father out of jail. I also suspected she lied to my father about her age. She would develop a lifelong habit of doing just that.

Reportedly, my parents met on a street corner. Street corners were the chat rooms of 1930s urban America. My mother would have been fourteen at the time, my father eighteen. Within a year or so of that first meeting, in October 1938, Bill and fifteen-year-old Fran eloped. After the marriage, they each continued to live at home until someone dropped a dime on the newlyweds. My father's utter likability and his Irish roots may well have saved his life. At six-foot-four, Granddad Purcell was huge by the standards of the day and surly when drunk.

My mother shocked friends and family by not having a baby soon after the wedding. By 1940, Fran and Bill were living on West Market Street, a mixed-ethnic commercial corridor a few blocks south of where my mother grew up. The young couple lived on the third floor of a seven-unit apartment building right next to the Carnival Club, home to the fabulous Boom Boom Room.

On April 4 of that year, the census taker came calling. We know that he spoke to Fran as he put an "x" next to her name, signifying he saw her. He also put an "x" next to the name of the couple's four-month-old son, Thomas. The census guy recorded that my mother was eighteen years old and had a high school degree. He listed my father as a twenty-year-old welder for the Ediphone company. The facts about my father are accurate save for a telling one, his age. In fact, he was a month shy of his twenty-second birthday at the time. Those concerning my mother are false in every detail.

As mentioned, Mom had a habit of fudging her age and other personal details. She had just turned seventeen at the time and had not graduated from high school. In fact, she never even attended high school. As to baby Thomas, that is pure mystery. When the 1940 census came online in 2012—the National Archives releases a given census seventy-two years after the fact—we were shocked to learn of this phantom brother. As a kid, I never heard a word about him, never sensed his absence.

In 2012, the only person who could confirm his existence was my mother's brother Bob, who was twelve in 1940 and close to my mother. Eighty-four and sharp when the 1940 census was released, Uncle Bob laughed at the news about our new brother Tom. There was no such kid, he assured us. We believed him.

Our mother had apparently borrowed a baby to fool the census taker. The only question was why. My best guess is her fear of the draft. Although Congress did not declare war until December 1941, the US instituted its first peacetime draft in September 1940. Talk of a draft had been in the air since war broke out in Europe in September 1939. Five days after the census taker came to West Market Street, Germany invaded Norway and Denmark. The "phony war" was over. Germany would attack Western Europe a month later.

A scam artist from the get-go, Fran, I am convinced, was trying to keep Bill out of the draft. Not only did she recruit a baby, but she also lopped a year off my father's age, knowing that the minimum age for a draftee would be twenty-one. The census ploy did not succeed. On October 16, 1940, the six-foot-tall William Ferdinand Cashill registered for the draft, listing as his employer "Thomas Edison." The legendary inventor had died a decade earlier at his West Orange, New Jersey, home, but the studio in that same city remained productive.

The idea that Newark and cities like it collapsed because employers left the central city overlooks the fact that many businesses had never been there or had left long before anyone heard the expression "White flight." For the first couple of years on the job, Bill would have taken the 21 Orange bus line from in front of his house on West Market Street to the Edison studios. The trip would have taken about a half hour. His father had worked for Edison as well. The radium girls took buses to their work in Orange once the company left Newark in 1920. Before the government made work more or less optional, people had no choice but to go where the jobs were. They felt an obligation to *make* a living.

In 1941, my parents bought their first car, a black 1935 Chevrolet. That same year, they had their first real child, William Francis Cashill, "Billy," my forever big brother. Although the "F" carried over, my parents were savvy enough to lose my father's middle name, the Germanic and bullish "Ferdinand." My mother's mother meanwhile insisted on being called "Ma." At thirty-seven, she thought herself a tad too young for "Grandma." Generations turned over quickly in that more reproductive age.

Together, Bill and Fran were living better than they ever had as children. Each of them grew up with an undependable father. (Yes, Virginia, the Irish men of that generation did drink. Stereotypes usually have roots in reality.) My brother Billy grew up in a much more stable household than his parents had. The Depression was over. Jobs were plentiful. And the future was bright—at least until December 7, 1941.

Our parents endured two phenomena that their baby boomer children never had to: a major depression and a world war. As much as they regaled us with tales of the former, they were oddly silent about the latter. And yet just about all young men went—quietly, dutifully, sometimes heroically. Not all of them returned. I was named after one who did not, my mother's cousin Jack Rogers, a Marine pilot lost in a Pacific typhoon. Every family, it seemed, had a Jack Rogers or two or three of its own.

Not one to volunteer for anything that did not involve family and friends, Bill waited to be called up. The Navy obliged him in 1943 and put his hard-earned vo-tech skills to work in the bowels of a tank-landing ship as anonymous as he was. Like many ships rolling off the assembly line late in the war, this one had no name. It went by the unmemorable designation, USS *LST-1086*. When the ship was commissioned on "24 February 1945," Bill was on board. According to official Navy history, "Following World War II, LST-1086 performed occupation duty in the Far East and saw service in China until late March 1946." As kids, Dad told us a little bit about China but a good deal more about being seasick. His red badge of courage came in a nasty shade of green.

JACK CASHILL

Ten months after the honorable discharge of Motor Machinist's' Mate Third Class William Cashill in February 1946, my brother Bob was born. I followed hot on Bob's heels eleven months later—"Irish twins." The same year I was born, my father applied for a job with the Newark Police Department. With many vets applying, he did well enough on the civil service exam to get one of the coveted spots. Driving him, like many young adults of that era, was the need for security. The Depression, which faded only with the outbreak of war in Europe, had left them all a little skittish.

I tell our story here not because it is exceptional, but because it is so typical of the working-class ethnics who peopled urban America. Their service during the war, on or off the front lines, was payback for the opportunity America afforded them. The nation rewarded them for that service with new opportunities in education and housing. A few years hence my grateful parents would take advantage of the latter.

Much too predictably, influential "antiracists" like Ibram X. Kendi see the GI Bill as something of a racist plot. From their perspective, just about everything is a racist plot. Such plots, real or imagined, keep the revenue flowing. Even during the COVID years, Kendi pulled in more than $300,000 per annum in "virtual" speaking fees.[18] As blue-collar philosopher Eric Hoffer reportedly observed some years back, "Every great cause begins as a movement, becomes a business, and eventually degenerates into a racket." Kendi's brand of antiracism skipped the first two phases. It was conceived as a racket.

Kendi was not exactly a hard-luck ghetto kid. Born Ibram Henry Rogers in 1982, Kendi attended a Christian primary school in Queens, New York, before his parents—his mother a business analyst, his father a tax accountant—moved to Virginia. Although Kendi attended a high school named after Stonewall Jackson, his Manassas district had long since moved on from its Confederate roots. If proof were needed, in 2000, the seventeen-year-old "Ibram Rogers" made the pages of the *Washington Post* for reaching the finals of the district-wide, tenth annual Martin Luther King Day oratorical contest.

A photo of Kendi headed the article, and the editors quoted a part of his speech. Assuming the role of King, Kendi had asked the thousand-strong audience, "How can [the dream] be over when kids know more about Puff Daddy than they know about me?"[19] Good question. In the years ahead, however, instead of seeking a solution to the cultural breakdown Puff Daddy represented, Kendi exploited it. Going forward, Kendi chose to blame systemic racism for just about everything, including the "model welfare system" of the GI Bill.

"Most urban Whites preferred 'flight over fight,'" writes Kendi in his bestseller *Stamped from the Beginning*. "Real estate agents, speculators, and developers benefitted selling fleeing Whites new suburban homes. America experienced an unprecedented post-war boom in residential and new highway construction as White families moved to the suburbs and had to commute farther to their jobs."[20] This racist caricature of post-war urban America may help Kendi sell books, but it bears little relation to reality.

Working class ethnics did not "flee" Newark with their new GI benefits. There was nothing to flee. In 1950, the city registered only twenty-four murders. Life was safe and orderly.

My family was still living at 384 West Market Street. Ours was a classic mixed-use neighborhood. To the immediate north of our back entrance on Littleton Avenue was a tavern. To the immediate south was an auto body shop whose scrapyard made a great playground for us and a parade of horrors for my mother. Directly across Littleton was a scissors factory whose compressors pounded our eardrums twenty-four hours a day. Along West Market Street were a small grocery, a butcher, and a baker. The grocer gave us kids a free pickle, the butcher a slice of bologna, the baker only the Proustian, memory-triggering smell of his shop. It still lingers.

Carrying two toddlers up three flights of stairs several times a day was a much more powerful incentive to find a new home than was the presence of a Chinese family in our building or a Black family in the building next door. Indeed, one of my earliest memories is of my father hammering a 4x4 into place over the existing back porch rail to keep us from tumbling over. That's what fathers did in Newark back then. They kept their kids from tumbling over.

STRAIGHT AND NARROW

J
ust about the time my parents moved to the apartment on West Market, six-year-old Amiri Baraka, then Leroy Jones, moved with his family to an apartment on Dey Street, about a fifteen-minute walk from our place. Writes Baraka in his 1987 autobiography, "This last move took us into the West (literally the West Ward) and a place where the Black community trailed off in a sputter of Italians."

An acute observer of social nuance, Baraka writes about this "standoff" with little rancor. "We were friends and enemies in the non-final cauldron of growing up," he observes. "We said things—did things—were things—and even became some other things that maybe could be understood on those streets, ca. 1940s."[21] I could have written about my own coming of age in much the same way.

One other African American chronicler of midcentury Newark, Emily "Cissy" Drinkard, lived in a neighborhood not unlike Amiri's but on the far side of town. "Our apartment, at 199 Court Street was in the middle of a racially mixed working-class neighborhood," writes Cissy, who was born in 1933, a year before Baraka. "It had its rough edges, but there were also churches on every corner."[22] Cissy's White neighbors tended to be Germans or Jews. She, too, writes about her early years among Whites without anger or bitterness.

Like the great majority of Blacks of their generation, both Cissy and Amiri grew up in strong, two-parent households. In both cases, their parents left the Jim Crow South in a spontaneous exodus known as the "Great Migration." This transition had the potential to be as disorienting as migration from overseas, but both sets of parents arrived in Newark with their values intact.

Baraka's father, Roy Jones, worked for the post office, and his mother as a hospital administrator. "My father and mother I knew and related to every which way I can remember," Baraka writes. "They were the definers of my world. My guides. My standards."[23]

Cissy writes lovingly of her parents as well. Of her mother, Delia Mae, she notes that only three things mattered to her: "God, her husband, and her children." She adds, "I never heard her complain, even though it was a constant struggle to keep eight kids neat, clean, and well-fed on my father's Depression-era salary of eighteen dollars a week." Nicholas Drinkard worked hard for that salary in the "blazing hot-foundry" of the Singer sewing machine factory in nearby Elizabeth.[24] I suspect Nicholas took a bus or two to get there from his Newark home. With one out of every four Americans jobless at the depth of the Depression, he was happy to have the work.

Nicholas took his job as father even more seriously than his position at Singer. "He was determined to protect his children from corruption and temptations, so he kept a close eye on us, requiring us to be home before dark and say our prayers before every meal," writes Cissy. "He wanted all his children to have strong Christian faith and walk the straight and narrow path as he had."[25]

Of the two young Newarkers, Cissy had the rougher go. While still a little girl, her mother suffered a disabling stroke. Like my Gramps, her father would carry his wife wherever she had to go. On Sunday, this meant down three flights of stairs to a waiting wheelchair, then over to church, and finally up three flights of stairs. "Seeing my parents' example," observes Cissy, "I grew up believing that no matter the hardship, you can overcome it with determination."[26]

Soon after her mother's stroke, Cissy watched helplessly as fire consumed an entire row of tenement houses, her apartment included. "Strangely," writes Cissy, the fire was a "godsend." The family found a new apartment in a more congenial mixed-race neighborhood in the vicinity of St. Luke's AME Church. "St. Luke's was more than just the place our family went to church," writes Cissy. "It was the place where my brothers and sisters and I learned to sing."[27] If faith sustained Cissy through a lifetime of travails—her mother died soon after the move—music gave her wings.

After a short-lived first marriage, Cissy found more secure footing with her second husband, John Houston Jr. The 1940 census found the nineteen-year-old John Jr. living with his father, John Sr., and his mother, Elizabeth. John Sr. worked as an engineer and wife Elizabeth as a trainer with the public schools. They lived at 205 Second Street in Roseville about a half mile from Myrtle Avenue.

I cite these details for a reason. Among the Roseville people I interviewed for this book was a fellow named Dave who was a year ahead of me at St. Rose. Late in the interview I asked if, when he was in school, there were any Black families living on his street. He said there was one. "Their little girl," he tells me, "went on to become a famous singer."

"Dionne Warwick?" I ask.

"No."

"Whitney Houston?"

"Yeah," he answers. "That's it."

I bought Cissy Houston's 2013 memoir, *Remembering Whitney*, to confirm Dave's memory. Unfortunately I could not confirm it, at least not exactly. Whitney Houston, who was born in 1963, never lived in Dave's neighborhood. Reviewing the 1940 census, however, I discovered that Whitney's grandfather, John Houston, did live on Dave's block. In a close-knit family like the Houstons, Whitney was likely a regular visitor. "We all got along with them," says Dave of the Houstons. The block remained stable for years. Even after the riots, even as the neighborhood deteriorated, Dave's parents stuck it out. His mother lived there until she died in 2007. At the end, the street was a war zone, his mother's house all but unsellable. "I shuddered driving down there," says Dave.

To draw conclusions about midcentury Newark from two memoirs is risky, but both Baraka and Cissy Houston suggest their experiences were not at all unique. Newark circa 1950 placed surprisingly few obstacles in the upward path of African Americans. Baraka's observations have particular value because he argues "against interest." As an adult, he did not exactly conceal his loathing of White people.

Three years before *Brown v. Board of Education* and a dozen years before the 1964 Civil Rights Act, Barringer High was well integrated. Baraka was one of four African Americans in his senior home room of twenty-nine, and one of ten students not obviously of Italian descent. Barringer could be a rough place for non-Italians, even for Italians, but especially so for Blacks. "I put up with many nigger callings and off the wall comments and intimidations, even getting cussed out regularly in Italian," Baraka writes. "But I tried to hold my own." He recounts no instance of violence.

"Embarrassed" by his height, or lack of it, Baraka fought back with humor. His fellow students took note. "His carefree and jovial manner has lighted many of our classrooms," say the editors of Baraka's senior yearbook. In his memoir, Baraka reports that he ran track and cross country, but he fails to mention that he was in the science club and the Latin Honor Society, neither affiliation worth much in the way of street cred. Upon graduation, he was offered a four-year scholarship to Seton Hall University and lesser scholarships to Holy Cross and Rutgers Newark.

His Black friends were moving up and out as well. Most of them went to my father's alma mater, Central High, "a technical and commercial high school." From his perch in 1987 as a celebrated Black nationalist and "goddam poet," Baraka writes dismissively of his friends' work experiences—"auto plants, utilities, electronic tube factories, mechanics, white-collar paper shuffling, teachers, small businessmen, security guards, commercial artists."[28] He misses, however, the obvious point: in post-war America, these were solid, respectable jobs. His friends were on the move. Jews excepted, Blacks were doing nearly as well as any ethnic group in midcentury Newark.

Unlike Cissy Houston, who embraced her parents' belief in America and their legacy of faith, Baraka rejected both. In the years ahead he would do his level best to destroy Newark, America for that matter. And for all his gifts as a wordsmith, he could never quite explain why.

JANITRESS

The year Amiri Baraka started his college days at Rutgers Newark, I started my academic career in the kindergarten of St. Rose of Lima. I was four years old. There were a lot of kids my age in 1952. The awkward but astonishing headline of a *Newark Star-Ledger* article on my kindergarten class makes this abundantly clear: "Nun loves care of 148 kids daily." As reporter Ruth Grosman explained, Sister Matthew Joseph "singlehandedly" tends to her "little learners," seventy-four in the morning, seventy-four in the afternoon.[29]

My eleven-year-old brother, Billy, walked me and Bob to school most mornings. The trip took us nearly fifteen minutes and involved crossing two major streets. Once my mother learned she was pregnant, my parents knew it was time to move. So late in the summer of 1953, as Baraka was preparing to transfer to Howard University, my father found an apartment at the top of Myrtle Avenue that was closer to the school—just three minutes on foot—and closer to the ground as well. Better still, this coal-fired second-floor unit did not have a back porch for us to tumble off of.

Myrtle Avenue ran one way south to north from Sussex Avenue to Orange Street, just one block. Its housing stock was as diverse as that of any single street in America: faux-elegant apartments, semi-trashy apartments, single-family homes, duplexes, triplexes, row houses, and one funky old grocery store in midblock, Shawger's by name. In 1950, immigrants from fourteen countries lived on Myrtle but no Blacks. By the time we arrived in 1953, three Black families lived in the triplex next door to us. In time, thanks to my paper route, I knew everyone who lived on the street. According to the 1950 census, "everyone" added up to 363 people.

In this era, working-class people of all races married and usually stayed married. In 1950, there were eighty-three married couples on Myrtle, seventy-nine of them with an employed male "head" of household. Two of those not employed were retired; two others were unemployed. Two widows also headed households, and twenty "roomers," mostly male, lived on the block as well. Of the seventy-nine households with a working male head, thirty also had a working female spouse. Today, I suspect, many blocks in Newark cannot boast of a single male married head of household.

The first immigrants to settle metropolitan New York, the Dutch, made at least one lasting contribution to the local patois, the word "stoop." Every residence on the block had a stoop—some small, some pretty epic like the one that fronted our triplex. We often played a game in which we threw a pink high-bouncer off the stoop, hoping to propel the ball across the narrow, lightly trafficked one-way street. We called the game, cleverly enough, "off the stoop." We probably inherited the game from the Dutch.

In a world without air-conditioning, people congregated on the stoops as soon as the weather permitted. The narrowness of the street encouraged adults to communicate with the neighbors across it. No one retreated to their back yards, as suburbanites famously do, because few of us had a backyard to retreat to. Besides, the front was where the action was.

"There must be eyes upon the street, eyes belonging to those we might call the natural proprietors of the street," writes Jane Jacobs in her classic work, *The Death and Life of Great American Cities*.[30] On Myrtle Avenue, there were lots of eyes and many natural proprietors. Better still, in a neighborhood like ours with more than a few shift workers, someone was inevitably sitting on his or her stoop at any time of day.

If Baraka moved to the street in 1953, when we did, he would have had little luck finding a college man to rap with about Frantz Fanon, Antonio Gramsci, or his other radical favorites. Even with the GI Bill, college was not in the cards for working men with families. Based on the occupations listed in the 1950 census, I doubt if there was a single college graduate on Myrtle. Short of lumberjack, the reader will be hard-pressed to identify a blue-collar job not represented on this hardworking block:

> Retired fireman
> Assembly work
> Truck driver
> Packer
> Janitor
> Janitress

Glazier
Machinist
Assistant office manager
Clerk
Foreman
Traffic clerk
Diet kitchen
Motor repairer
Reports clerk
Radio assembler
Cashier
Waitress
Typist
Electric winding
Toolmaker
Manager (shoe store)
Machine maintenance
Auto body work
Watchman
Porter
Public accountant
Casket maker
Pipe fitter
Tool & die maker
Bartender
Crimper, medical
Engineer
Butcher
Storekeeper

Secretary
Plumbing and heating
Bookkeeper
Tavern proprietor
Carpenter
Motor inspector
Printing
Chief clerk
Teacher, parochial school
Painter (auto)
Stock clerk
Utility man
Beltmaker
Warehouse supervisor
Stenographer
Dental hygienist
Clerk, office
Trolley operator
Telephone operator
Retired policemen
Home typist
Chauffeur
Auto repair foreman
Order clerk
Laborer
Beautician
Soda clerk
Assistant stylist
Practical nurse

Machine operator
Rubber molder
Stenotyper
Social worker, Catholic Charities
Electrician
Salesman
Electrical repair
Kitchen help
Office clerk
Fireman
Stationary engineer
Inspector
Undertaker
Sales clerk
Seamstress
Baker
Powder manufacturer
Maintenance
Cutter
City employee
Army Air Corp
Saleslady
Bus driver
Housekeeper
Parkway worker
Hoisting engineer
Matron
Salesman (lighting)
Cook

Accountant
Radio operator
Aircraft machinist
Plater
Motor switchman
Shipper
Painter
Short order cook
Counter clerk
Sales
General manager (employment office)
Huckster (vegetables)
"On compensation"
Elevator operator
Counterman
Guard
Maintenance man
Super
Maintenance engineer

Other than perhaps casket maker, the occupation that made me smile most was "janitress." This was a woman who embraced her sex and took pride in her work. Note, too, that very few of these jobs involved working for a large manufacturer. The idea has been floated ad infinitum that the collapse of Newark and other industrial cities was caused by the loss of major manufacturers. As shall be seen, this claim does not rise to the level of half-truth.

Even more dubious is Kendi's claim that the GI Bill was a welfare program and a racist one at that. The men, Black and

White, who gave up years of their lives to the service of their country, might object to the word "welfare." The reward for that service was minimal. As amended in 1945, the VA home loan program guaranteed loans for vets only up to $4,000 and gave them ten years from war's end to make their move. With growing families and limited incomes, few young working-class couples could afford to buy any kind of house anywhere, VA loan or no. As a result, on Myrtle Avenue in 1953, only a handful of nuclear families lived without relatives or boarders in a home they owned. Many extended families doubled and tripled up.

In 1954, with the ten-year clock running down, my parents made their move. More prudent than most, they put a bid in on a $7,000 home. They did not go "sprawling into the subdivided woods," as antiracist guru Ta-Nehisi Coates imagined they would. They bought an 1880s-vintage fixer-upper halfway down the street, number 29 Myrtle to be precise. An elderly female boarder came with the house. We would live there for the next ten years.

In "The Case for Reparations," an overpraised article in *The Atlantic*, Coates argues that housing segregation wasn't simply the work of individual home owners. It was instead the intended result of government policy. "White flight," he insists, "was not an accident—it was a triumph of racist social engineering."[31] This isn't sociology. This is conspiracy theory. The government has always been more clumsy than clever. In Roseville, the authorities would socially engineer us out of our homes in the near future simply because we were in the way.

Reading Coates's books and articles, I get no sense that he has ever spoken to a working-class White person. To be sure, none were quoted in the reparations article. Born in 1975 to a radical family—his father, Paul Coates, had been a Black Panther—young Coates did not have to wander far from home to find his ideology. Paul Coates ran Black Classic Press, a radical publishing house. Coates's mother was a school teacher and one of the four women who bore Paul Coates his seven children.

Like Amiri Baraka, Coates attended Howard University but never got around to graduating. Degrees were for lesser mortals than Baraka and Coates. In the age of forced diversity, editors were keen to hire a smart guy like Coates regardless of his credentials. In 2008, his life took a profitable turn when he dared to write an article attacking the not yet fallen Black icon Bill Cosby, then in his conservative "pull up your pants" phase.

"His historical amnesia—his assertion that many of the problems that pervade black America are of a recent vintage—is simply wrong," writes the thirty-something Coates of the seventy-something Cosby.[32] The article helped ease anxiety among do-gooding Whites who feared their own misguided policies may have caused Black decline. Having found his audience, Coates shifted his career into full-time antiracism. In the years since, few have mined this mother lode more productively.

In 2019, before the COVID shutdown, Coates delivered the inaugural "Distinguished Diversity Lecture" at Ohio State University. This was a typical gig for the woke rock star.

Adding in the first-class airfare, per diem, lodging at a four-star hotel, and private transportation, the hour-long event cost OSU $41,500.[33] When last I checked, Coates had a net worth of $6 million. Coates, it would seem, has gotten his own running head start on reparations.

TRAIL OF TEARS

n 1953, the year we moved to Myrtle Avenue, refugees were streaming into Roseville, some from Europe, of course, but some, too, from our adjoining neighborhood to the east, the old First Ward. In July of that year, bulldozers had begun leveling not just the homes of these refugees but their bakeries, their butcher shops, their groceries, their restaurants, and the very streets at the heart of Newark's "Little Italy," one of the largest Italian communities in North America.

The First Ward refugees moved more or less seamlessly into Roseville. By the early 1950s, the resistance to Italians from the earlier-arriving ethnic groups, especially the Irish, had eased considerably. The Catholic Church had much to do with assimilating new arrivals, especially through its schools. That said, when my mother's brother Bob brought Lucille Bonoumo home to meet the parents in 1947, Granddad Purcell was less than thrilled. The story went that Granddad threatened to boycott the wedding, but there is no one left to verify that. My future aunt Lucille, the rare woman of that era to own her own car, brought me home from the hospital when I was born later that year, and we remained close to the end.

Racism played no role in the Italian exodus from Little Italy. Eminent domain did the job, much the same tool the government used to send the Cherokee on their trail of tears a century or so earlier. As Michael Immerso tells the story in his colorful and definitive book, *Newark's Little Italy: The Vanished First Ward*, southern Italians had settled in the neighborhood as early as 1873. Within a decade, they numbered more than a thousand.

As is often true of newcomers anywhere, the Italians were not necessarily well received. In 1881, a weekly Newark publication, the *Sentinel of Freedom*, gave these newly minted Americans something of a mixed review. "Though the Italians form a very small part of the population of Newark," opined the *Sentinel*, "they are steadily growing in numbers and, as a rule, are quiet, inoffensive people, and many of them are industrious and thrifty and are steadily making money." So far, so good, then this unfiltered gem: "They come chiefly from Naples and a more ragged, dirty set of people it would be hard to imagine."[34]

Italians, from my experience, are less inclined to dwell on past injustices than most other ethnic groups. They have not, for instance, pounded into our consciousness the events that took place in New Orleans in 1891. They could have. That year the city's popular police chief was shot down on a city street. As the chief lay dying, he was asked who shot him. He reportedly whispered, "Dagoes."

Nine Italians were rounded up for trial. In a tribute to American justice, the jury found six of the accused innocent and could not reach a verdict on the guilt of the other three. As happens even today, unpopular verdicts provoke mobs to violence. In this case, on March 14, 1891, a mob stormed the jail and lynched the nine accused, plus two of their *paisanos* who got in the way.[35] This attack represented the most deadly mass lynching in American history. Life was rough all over in 1891, and America was still working through its imperfections.

Rather than fret about systemic racism, just a year after the New Orleans lynchings Italians proudly celebrated the four hundredth anniversary of Christopher Columbus's discovery of America. In Newark, some thirty-two Italian societies joined in the festivities. For Italians, no historical figure solidified their status as real Americans the way Columbus did. In 1927, with the cooperation of the city, Newark's Italians chipped in to build an epic statue of Christopher Columbus in downtown's Washington Park. Some fifty thousand people showed up for a parade and the unveiling.

By the 1920s, thirty thousand people lived in the First Ward, twenty thousand of them either foreign-born or first-generation Italian or Sicilian. To speak of America today as more diverse than ever is to ignore the early twentieth century. Before the age of mass communication, immigrants arrived with minimal knowledge of America or its culture. Save for the Irish, most couldn't speak a lick of English. They looked strange, dressed strange, even smelled strange, and natives felt free to tell them just how strange they seemed.

Despite the obstacles, the Italians of Newark did well, and Little Italy reflected their progress. In the years following the Depression and World War II, Eighth Avenue, Little Italy's main drag, bustled with nightclubs, new restaurants, and shops of all sorts. St. Lucy's Roman Catholic Church, the heart of the community, pulled the neighborhood together, and the street festivals, writes Immerso, "were as elaborate and as boisterous as ever."[36] Incredibly, within just a few years, Eighth Avenue and the culture it supported would be wiped from the map.

To help me with my research, I asked a veteran police officer and old family friend—we'll call him Mario—to show me Newark as it exists today. Mario was armed. He would not have ventured into these neighborhoods unarmed. One of the sites we visited was St. Lucy's. It stands today as regal and imposing as it did when built nearly a century ago.

A few years back, I attended a wedding at the church. The bride, of course, was Italian. The church remains the spiritual center of the Italian diaspora. Like many Italian Americans of her generation, she chose St. Lucy's over the suburban parish church in which she came of age. She chose well. The sheer majesty of the interior elevated the ceremony and sanctified the relationship. To this day, many young marrieds and others return to the church in October for the procession honoring St. Gerard Majella, a pious eighteenth-century Italian revered as the patron saint of expectant mothers.

The low-rise, low-income housing surrounding St. Lucy's is as bleak and banal as St. Lucy's is grand. "It doesn't look terrible," I said to Mario.

"You should see the insides," he said. "I've been here on too many calls." How Little Italy came to so inglorious an end so quickly is a story that needs sharing. It was not the first time in urban America that corrupt schemers collaborated with clueless dreamers to destroy a neighborhood. Nor would it be the last.

Some background is in order. On April 30, 1950, two thousand people packed St. Lucy's, and thousands of gawkers filled the streets around the church to catch sight of the celebrities, criminal and otherwise, attending the wedding of Tony Boy Boiardo, the son and heir of Capo Richie "the Boot" Boiardo. Among the thousand guests invited to the wedding reception—no one in Newark has ever worried about "optics"—were Newark Mayor Ralph Villani, a Republican, and Congressmen Hugh Addonizio and Peter Rodino, both Democrats.[37]

More than twenty years after the Boiardo wedding, Rodino would emerge as a media darling for his role as chairman of the House Judiciary Committee during the Watergate hearings. In Rodino's *New York Times* obituary, Michael Kauffman quoted the congressman as saying of the Watergate inquiry, "I know we're sometimes weak-kneed, and sometimes political. But I really believe this is an instance when we can demonstrate that the system does work."[38] In 1952, he and Mayor Villani showed just how the system can work against the people it was designed to serve. For conflicting reasons, they collaborated on the destruction of Rodino's own neighborhood.

In his defense, Rodino was a true believer in urban redevelopment. The *New York Times* shared the details of his dream for Little Italy in a June 1952 article whose headline had to appall every literate resident therein, "Big Newark Slum to Be Housing Site." Apparently, the federal government took some time off from its "racist social engineering" to plan the eviction of more than three thousand White people from their "slum." The plan called for the destruction of 477 buildings, most of them three-story walk-ups. Replacing these structures would be eight thirteen-story, low-rent apartment houses of two hundred units each. "They told us our homes were slums," one neighbor told Immerso. "They weren't slums."[39]

The "housers," as they actually called themselves, saw things otherwise. Beginning with the creation of the Federal Housing Authority (FHA) during the first rush of FDR's New Deal, the federal government had begun to play an active role in housing America. The housers had a cultish belief in the power of buildings to transform lives. The housers of the FHA invited cities to establish local housing authorities that the federal government would help fund. The idea of spending someone else's money was as seductive for local pols then as it is today.

There was, however, a catch. To build new housing units, the housing authority had to demolish a comparable number of "slum dwellings." With dollar signs clouding their vision, local officials began to see slums wherever they looked. Black author James Baldwin's 1963 comment that urban renewal "means Negro removal"[40] has been quoted often enough to become folklore, but the latter day critics of urban renewal fail to understand the spirit of the times. At every stage of the process, progressives paved the road to urban hell with their good intentions, and it did not matter what ethnic group they had to steamroll to get the job done.

On paper, the Columbus Homes project sounded promising. "Widespread interest in the project has been shown in business and commercial circles," reported the *Times* uncritically, "because it combines public housing and private development."[41] Public-private partnerships meant one thing in the minds of the nation's social engineers. These partnerships meant something altogether different on the streets of Newark. The more money the federal government pumped into local government, the more powerful it made the public officials distributing that money.

Failing to see how federal government overreach deforms local politics—or not caring—DiAngelo, Coates, Kendi, and other antiracists remain champions of big government. They should pay more attention. If Villani had asked locals to pony up their own tax dollars for the Columbus Homes, they would have laughed him out of office. Thanks to the feds, however, Newark politicians were now playing with house money.

It is possible, if unlikely, that Rodino failed to anticipate what was to come. Some powerful people approved the project in all innocence. Most notable among them was St. Lucy's formidable pastor, Father Gaetano Ruggiero. A strong-willed Sicilian, Ruggiero nevertheless fell for the snake oil. "He was sold a bill of goods," his successor, Monsignor Granato, told Immerso. "He thought the people could stay and have better homes. By the time he fully understood the enormity of the project, it was too late. When he saw that people were thrown out against their will, unable to return, he couldn't sleep for three years."[42]

Mayor Villani was another story. To push the plan through, he had to override the pleas of his own constituents, ignore their petitions, and fight their lawsuit. "May God strike me dead if I want to harm anyone," Villani told the protestors. "Nobody will be thrown out into the streets. Some day you people will build a monument to me for what I'm trying to do for this city."[43]

The oldest of ten children of an immigrant family, Villani grew up "down neck"—an industrial part of town more formally known as the Ironbound district. This was where the fictional Tony Soprano grew up as well. Ambitious to a fault, Villani graduated from law school, finessed his way through the minefields of Newark politics, and eventually got himself elected mayor in 1949. On the way to the top, Villani learned the art of the kickback and would be indicted for the same while running for reelection in 1953, the year the demolition started. The headline of the *New York Times* article reads today like boilerplate, "Mayor of Newark Denies Kickbacks."[44] Villani was unrepentant.

At ground zero of the demolition site was Vittorio Castle, a neighborhood landmark. Boiardo and a partner had opened this absurdly ornate restaurant in 1937. For some years Boiardo entertained friends and gangster allies here, as well as celebrities like Joe DiMaggio, Jack Dempsey, and George Raft. Given his investment in the community and his sway over its politicians, Boiardo had both the motive and the power to block the destruction of his old neighborhood. He chose not to. Like Villani, he saw the future in public housing. With his connections to the city's labor unions and the construction trades, Boiardo could all but count the dollars buried in a $40 million project with many more such projects to come. Boiardo took special interest since he just so happened to have started a demolition company with the not at all subtle name, "Boiardo Construction."

Vittorio Castle had outlived its shelf life in any case. Television was reshaping the way people spent their leisure hours, and the various scandals surrounding the castle were driving legitimate business away. The government was sure to pay Boiardo above market value if for no other reason than to keep him from leading a popular resistance from behind castle walls. Instead, Boiardo used the now moribund castle as his office while Boiardo Construction helped raze Little Italy.[45]

The construction work itself was just part of the Boiardo master plan. If not in 1953, certainly a decade later during the tenure of Mayor Hugh Addonizio, the Boiardos would take a slice out of just about every construction contract to come out of city hall, most of them federally funded. So, too, would Addonizio. Years later, a government informant asked Addonizio why he left a soft congressional job in Washington for the mess back home. "Simple," Addonizio answered. "There's no money in Washington, but you can make a million bucks as mayor of Newark."[46]

I asked my police friend Mario if he thought Little Italy might still be thriving if Boiardo had gone to bat for its residents. He thought that scenario entirely plausible. For Boiardo, Little Italy was real estate to be exploited. He no longer lived anywhere near the First Ward. A 1957 FBI report described where he did live: "Boiardo resides in a castle like house set back from the road and nearly hidden from view by a high stonewall."[47] The setting was the still semi-rural Livingston, New Jersey, about fifteen miles west of Little Italy. Boiardo had bought a thirty-acre property there in 1939 and moved from Newark in 1945. Apparently, he liked castles.

The residents of Little Italy did not have that kind of mobility. The demolition of the neighborhood began in July 1953 and continued in stages for the next three years. "Uprooted families felt profound grief, as if mourning a loved one who had passed away too soon," writes Immerso. The accounts of their forced departure echoed the lamentations of my ancestors forced out of Ireland.

"When they built Columbus Homes, they tore us apart," one resident told Immerso. "It was a disaster. It broke people's hearts," said another. "It wasn't a choice," said a third. "You had to get out."

Immerso writes poignantly of the fallout: "Grandparents, aunts, and uncles who lived together under the same roof suddenly had to find new homes. Scores of family-owned businesses that thrived in the neighborhood were forced out and very few ever reopened."

If the young could adapt, many of the elderly could not. With friends and family scattered and familiar shops shuttered, despair swept the surrounding neighborhood as cholera once had. "They were heartbroken," a former resident told Immerso. "A few months later you read their names in the obituaries."[48] In August 1955, Columbus Homes opened to much fanfare, and soon enough even Rodino began to recognize the monster he helped midwife.

The dad of a Newark friend was Rodino's cousin and a one-time resident of Little Italy. "My father was devastated by what happened," Ken tells me. "He was astonished by Rodino. He always thought he was a straight ahead guy. I have no idea what deals were made."

Said Rodino after the damage had been done, "I felt we could improve. We visualized people coming into quarters that were up-to-date. The original design for Columbus Homes looked like a dream to me."[49] To say that the dream turned into a nightmare may sound a bit trite, but there is no better word to describe the darkness that befell Columbus Homes.

FREE RANGE

The same month that the demolition began in Little Italy, and just about a mile away, we moved to Myrtle Avenue. I was oblivious to the drama unfolding just down the road. Our drama was at home. My mother was pregnant when we moved, and to my father's unconcealed delight, she gave birth to a girl. The date was December 17, 1953, two days after my sixth birthday.

Maureen's arrival proved to be liberation day for my brother and me. Now with my mother preoccupied, we could go wherever we chose. This freedom was not unique to us or to our friends. Kids all over the country, urban and rural, in small towns and in big cities, walked or biked or even bused wherever they pleased. "We were free-range kids," a grade-school classmate reminds me while providing some hair-raising examples from his own childhood. In fact, boomers often regale their children with talk of that era's freedom forgetting we were the ones who pulled in the reins on our own kids.

My mother turned thirty before my sister was born. Having four children was close to the neighborhood median at the time. With so many kids on the block and so many responsible parents, my mother relied on the stoop-sitters and window-watchers throughout the neighborhood and beyond to keep an eye on us. If we went seriously astray, the neighbor-hood tom-toms would have alerted my mother before we got home. "All of our parents knew each other," my schoolmate Frank recalls, "and no one got bent out of shape if an adult told you to quiet down or not to sit on their car."

Stoop culture had one major drawback. The people who sat on stoops weren't always the people you wanted sitting on them. In the way of backstory, the first two years on Myrtle we lived at the top of the block directly across the street from "the apartments," a cluster of three large buildings, each with about twenty units. On Sunday mornings, my brother Billy would give me a nickel to help deliver his newspapers. I would run the papers up the stairs and through the musty, overheated halls of these weary buildings, sensing even then that something had gone wrong in the lives of the people who lived there.

In doing the research for this project I heard from Mike, a funny guy a few years older than I who lived in these apart-ments. More humbly still, he lived with his immigrant parents and four siblings in a basement unit. On our block, life didn't get much lower, literally or metaphorically.

An easy guy to talk to, I asked Mike what unhappy fate had consigned his family to that netherworld. "The Irish plague," he laughs. "My father changed jobs a lot, which was why we lived in a basement." He knew I would need no expla-nation about the "plague" nor take offense.

Irish American males of that generation drank a lot. Both my grandfathers were tipplers. If alcoholism is a "disease," I have a hard time understanding why my grandfathers did not pass that gene along to their descendants. In fact, they were situational drunks. The tavern simply provided an easy escape from small apartments swelling with kids. Some men yielded to its temptations. Some did not. Mike's father yielded. "Even though my dad had a problem with booze," Mike adds, "my mother stuck with him."

His mom's resolution made all the difference. His father eventually abandoned the bottle, and the family's fortunes improved. His parents never stopped teaching their kids the virtue of hard work. "You had to work for everything," says Mike. "That's what my folks told us." He and all his siblings took the message to heart. All have done well in life, some "very well." Like the rest of us, though, they have no neighborhood to return to, no stoops to revisit.

I still remember the guys who hung out on the apartment stoops. I ran their names by Mike—Clancy, Rollo, Butchie. I think of them collectively as Cerberus, the mythical multiheaded hound of Hades that guarded the gates of the Underworld. Mike confirmed these were not just goblins haunting my imagination. They were real-life goons. He knew them all. To access Myrtle Avenue and the world beyond, I had to get by them.

In addition to being the last of the free-range children, boomers, generously defined, were the last cohort of young people to share a fully common culture. With only a few regional variations, we all watched the same TV shows, saw the same movies, listened to the same music, and had the same heroes. In his Vietnam classic, *Full Metal Jacket*, director Stanley Kubrick captured the universality of boomer culture when he has his US Marines march off to battle singing the theme song to *The Mickey Mouse Club*. On watching the scene, I was tempted to sing along.

In the mid-1950s, the hero of every red-blooded American boy was Davy Crockett. The avuncular Walt Disney shared Crockett's exploits over five, wildly popular one-hour episodes in 1954 and 1955. The theme song from Davy Crockett quickly reached number one on the top-forty charts, and we could all sing it, word for word.

As my First Communion present in 1955, I asked for a Davy Crockett suit. Of course I did. My mother tried to talk me into a watch, arguing that I would wear the suit once or twice and then deep-six it, but I wasn't budging. Having put her payment down on a future "I told you so," my mother relented and bought a Davy Crockett suit for Bob as well.

Now I imagine there were streets all over America in which a seven-year-old could proudly venture out in his new Davy Crockett suit with the trademark coonskin cap and be met with envy and admiration. Myrtle Avenue just wasn't one of those streets. As soon as the hoods on the apartment stoop saw us, they descended. Within seconds, it seems, they had encircled Bob and me and started braying like jackasses, "Born on a mountaintop in Tennessee/ Greenest state in the land of the free…"

We didn't need to hear any more. We got the message. I never wore my Davy Crockett suit in public again. As I was learning, there was a rough edge to life on our block, just enough of an edge to slice the dork right out of us. For us to survive as free-range children in Newark, a little hardening was essential. On walking out the front door, we would have to leave our childish enthusiasms behind. When taunted, we would have to taunt back. When hit, we would have to fight back. If we didn't, our parents—to a person—would push us right back out into the street and insist we do.

One thing we had little of in our part of Roseville, close to none actually, was grass. I had heard there was a park in neighboring East Orange with an actual baseball diamond. So one Saturday morning, glove in hand, I decided to walk there by myself. Google Maps tells me it was about fifteen minutes on foot. Not knowing the way then, I am sure it took me longer.

About seven at the time, I had to be the youngest kid in the park. Of course, there were no adults present. There rarely were. For better or worse, kids managed their own lives. "We made up our own games," Brendan, a Pigs refugee, confirms. "We learned how to organize ourselves."

The choosing of sides began with an elaborate ritual in which one of the self-appointed captains tossed a bat to the other captain. Each would then put hand over hand on the bat hoping to be the last one to find wood enough to hold on to. If that captain could hang on to the bat when kicked, he got to choose first.

The choosing was all done publicly. The first few kids chosen swelled with pride as their names were called while the rest of us stood around anxiously. As the draft pool contracted, the chosen openly registered their disgust at the pickings that were left. On this morning, there were nineteen kids present. I was number nineteen. With the draft complete, the one captain looked at me, shrugged his shoulders, and said, "Get lost, kid."

I trudged home. The trip took me by Newk's, an all-Black bar on Orange Street just west of St. Rose. Dodger great Don Newcombe, then at the peak of his powers, owned the bar. I made note. My fellow Dodger fan Artie and I would come back periodically to get Newk's autograph. We would pass a piece of paper to the man at the door, and it would inevitably come back signed. Who signed it? We had no idea, but we convinced ourselves it was Newk.

We did not know it at the time, but Newk's life was heading into free fall. As he proved, owning a bar was not an ideal profession for an alcoholic. "I was a stupefied, wife-abusing, child-frightening, falling-down drunk," he would later confess.[50] At his nadir, in 1965, he pawned his World Series ring. As it happens, the collapse of his life almost perfectly paralleled that of the neighborhood around him. The walk I took at seven I would not have taken at seventeen. Nor would I take it today.

Much more accessible to us was another baseball legend, Moe Berg. The only problem is that we did not know he was there. In a very un-Jewish move, Berg put his law license to the side in 1923 and began his Major League Baseball career as a catcher with the Philadelphia Phillies. Known as the "brainiest man in baseball," he played and coached for a series of teams for the next eighteen years. Although he never became a star as Newcombe had—in fact, he was rarely a starter—Berg became a legend.

Berg owed his legendary status to his exploits during World War II. Thanks to his exceptional language skills and his extraordinary memory, Berg was recruited by the Office of Strategic Services, the OSS, a precursor to the CIA. In early 1944, the OSS sent Berg to Italy to encourage European physicists to defect to the United States. His primary target was Werner Heisenberg, Walter White's meth-making alias on *Breaking Bad*. Berg was reportedly tasked with killing Heisenberg if he thought Germany capable of building an atomic bomb.

Like many a returning veteran, Berg had a difficult time adjusting after the war. In 1947, broke and dispirited, he moved in with his doctor brother Sam on Roseville Avenue, two blocks from my house. For the next twenty-five years, in between occasional assignments with the CIA and side trips to sporting events, Berg wandered the neighborhood. For years, his favorite watering hole was Gruning's, the popular ice cream parlor a block from my house. He would sit at the counter and read for hours. I am sure I passed him at some point. If I had known who he was, I would have bugged him for an autograph.

To his good fortune, Newcombe's wife stood by him. So did the Dodgers. Thanks to their help, Newk turned his life around. Although not an alcoholic, Berg had problems that transcended easy recovery. In 1964, the ever-patient Dr. Sam finally asked his deadbeat brother to leave. His sister Ethel, who also lived in Roseville, took him in, more to spite Sam than to help Moe. Like the neighborhood around him, Berg was fading fast.

As kids, we explored the city much as Moe Berg did and with as little purpose. One day, Bob and I, along with Artie and broken-home Bobby, wandered into East Orange along the commuter railroad tracks that ran below street level through our neighborhood. Unseen from above, we lit little fires as we wandered. Our budding careers as arsonists came to an abrupt end when the East Orange police nabbed us. We were about to get off with a lecture when my brother un-cleverly mouthed off, "You can't arrest us. My father's a cop." That did it.

When alerted by the East Orange police, my father, although a reluctant executioner, reached into the closet for his thick black police belt. He had warned us never to play on the tracks, and we disregarded his warning. We deserved what was to come, almost welcomed it. We certainly preferred it to the probationary conditions my mother attached to our punishment: a month in the house, a year on the block. Of course, after a week of whining and groveling we were sprung, but we never went back to East Orange. What happens there doesn't stay there.

Ward Cleaver never took a belt to the Beaver, but I think he would have if Beaver had done what we did. The show *Leave It to Beaver* first aired on October 4, 1957. The Beaver, Jerry Mathers, and I were both nine years old at the time. When my friends and I watched the Cleaver family in its anodyne suburban redoubt, we did not see an alien world. We saw a world very much like our own, albeit a good deal dorkier.

Professional antiracist Tim Wise, who is himself White, doesn't get this. Like many in the antiracist biz, he seems obsessed with the Cleavers. The show speaks of a time, Wise says with attempted sarcasm, "when everything was in its place, before all the struggles for equality and justice came along in the 60s and messed everything up." Today, he imagines, "You have a whole political movement that is based on escaping into that fantasy."[51]

Condescending to his core, Wise insists that working-class Whites of the 1950s "wouldn't have wanted to watch something that was just like their actual life," but Wise knows nothing about our actual lives. My father was at least as wise and patient as Ward. Although she did not wear pearls, and worked part-time, my mother put dinner on the table seven nights a week. Like most women of Irish descent, she was savvy enough to abandon her ancestral cuisine, such as it was, when introduced to Italian food. I'm not sure what June prepared, but I am sure it was no match for my mother's Italian hot dogs or macaroni and meat.

Leave It to Beaver was no more a fantasy than, say, *The Honeymooners* or *The Life of Riley*, two popular shows with working-class characters that apparently did not fit Wise's narrative. *Leave It to Beaver* worked because its appeal was universal. If its setting was artificial, the show's values, traditions, and expectations mirrored those of most Americans, White and Black. Said Barack Obama of Michelle's family, "It turned out that visiting the Robinson household was like dropping in on the set of Leave It to Beaver."[52]

Twenty-five profitable years lecturing guilt-ridden White people has apparently made Wise an expert on White flight. In the world according to Wise, White flight "began as soon as communities and schools came to have even small numbers of people of color in them."[53] This is a remarkable observation in that it ignores very nearly *all* real-world evidence. In that same self-hating book, *Dear White America*, Wise insists, "Unless we grapple with the past in its fullness—and come to appreciate the impact of that past on our present moment—we will find it increasingly difficult to move into the future a productive, confident, and even remotely democratic republic."[54] If Wise is serious about grappling with the past, he might begin by speaking to those driven out of Roseville. Collectively, they just might be able to convince him that the sixties really did "mess everything up."

TABACHNIK'S
PICKLE BARRELS

"I can't recount what my grandfather went through when leaving the only home he and my grandmother lived in," writes one of my Facebook friends, "but this is one of the sad remnants of that diaspora." She linked to an article from 2008 that explored an ongoing Newark tradition, the "Day of Jewish Return."[55]

No single event speaks more vividly to the tragic irony of Newark's collapse than this mournful day, celebrated—if that's the right word—on a Sunday between the High Holy Days. On this one day alone do Jews feel safe enough to honor their dead. Law enforcement officers, almost all Jewish and volunteers, make this day possible by escorting mourners to their cemeteries. "It's absolutely sad to see what was once a great Jewish city come to the point where 200 Jews out of the 65,000 that once lived there have to come once a year with a police escort," said Warren Grover, a local historian. "It's sad, but it's life."[56]

The experience of Jews in Newark more closely parallels that of Jews in other northern cities than it does the experience of Newark's Irish and Italians. In the much-studied

North Lawndale section of Chicago, for instance, the racial transition was even swifter than in Newark. Despite a seeming "absence of inter-racial violence," the Jewish population in that neighborhood went from sixty-five thousand in 1946 to a "few hundred" by 1956.[57]

Alex, a Facebook friend from Detroit, tells a similar story about that city's Dexter-Davison area. He remembers a harmonious working-to-middle-class neighborhood that "basically collapsed" in the late 1950s. "Lieberman's closed," Alex writes. "The kosher butcher my mom patronized closed. Mr. Meisel's shoe store was gone." His older brother was "often shaken down for his lunch money," and his mother had her purse snatched several times in a two-month period. "We moved to the suburbs," he says regretfully.

Ironically, no ethnic group was more welcoming to the African Americans streaming into America's cities. The Jewish People's Institute of Chicago, for instance, took the initiative of organizing the North Lawndale Citizens Council, "which had racial integration as its goal."[58] I don't know of any other ethnic group organizing anything comparable anywhere in America. The North Ward Citizens' Committee of Newark, as shall be seen, had rather the opposite purpose.

In Newark, even without a welcoming committee, Blacks moved more readily into Jewish neighborhoods, sensing they would be better received than in Irish or Italian neighborhoods. All this is true, and yet no ethnic group fled more quickly than the Jews. In the final analysis, the distinct virtues of the Jewish community rendered that community uniquely vulnerable.

The virtues were many. So were the accomplishments. The great mass of Eastern European Jews flowed into Newark slightly before the Great Migration of African Americans, at roughly the same time as the Italians, and slightly after the Irish and the Germans. They joined the remnants of a German Jewish population that had come to Newark earlier in the nineteenth century. Whether from Eastern Europe or Germany, the arriving Jews spoke little, if any, English. Most showed up in Newark as poor as the gentile immigrants, and they were no more welcome, maybe less. Yet by mid-twentieth century, Jews had made a greater contribution to the arts and commerce of Newark than all the other ethnic groups combined.

William Helmreich, author of *The Enduring Community*, observes almost matter-of-factly, "As one indicator, we have only to look at the many well-known people for whom Newark was home in the formative years of their lives: Philip Roth, Edward Koch, Jerome Kern, Fanny Brice, Jerry Lewis, Dore Schary, Leslie Fiedler, and many, many more." As Helmreich adds, Jews made some notable contributions to industry and business as well: "Bamberger's, Ronson Lighter Company, Pathmark, Home Depot, Alpine Lace, and so on."[59]

Bamberger's, an epic department store, was central to the cultural life of the city. A German Jew, Louis Bamberger learned the dry goods business at his uncle's store in Baltimore. After considerable research, he saw his main chance in Newark. In 1892, in league with his two brothers-in-law, he bought out an existing store in the heart of downtown Newark and immediately began expanding. By 1924, Bamberger's employed twenty-eight hundred people.

To go there as a kid was to go someplace special. We had to dress up to go. My most enduring memory is riding up in the elevator and having the elevator operator announce the wonders that awaited us on each floor: "Fifth floor—furniture, bedding; seventh floor—housewares, kitchenware, gourmet shop." We bused down to Bamberger's every Christmas season, of course, to present Santa our list of demands. All other department store Santas struck us as counterfeit.

We did not think of Bamberger's as a Jewish store. In fact, as kids, we were not really conscious of the classification "Jew." In retrospect, I realize that many of the stores up and down Orange Street in Roseville were Jewish-owned including several I frequented like H&B's, where I bought my Hostess Snoballs, and Ratner's, the all-purpose candy store that sold us kids baseball cards and high-bouncers. I hear occasionally of Catholic school kids who taunted Jews as "Christ-killers." That may have been true somewhere but not in our world. I knew a whole lot of racial taunts—and confess to having fired off a few as warranted—but "Christ-killer" was not in my arsenal.

Unknown to me when young was the role Louis Bamberger played in Newark's cultural life. He donated the buildings for the Newark Museum and the New Jersey Historical Society. He acquired for the society a full set of autographs of the signers of the Declaration of Independence and gave the museum many art, archaeological, and scientific objects from his own collection. "I never doubted that this country was mine (and New Jersey and Newark as well)," Philip Roth would write.[60] The same sentiment reigned in our neighborhood. We never thought of ourselves as anything but true-blue Newarkers and Americans.

For all their contributions to American culture and their commitment to education, Jews failed to do one thing that the Irish and the Italians did—create their own schools. "Newark's Jews were particularly fortunate in that the Protestant elite, which controlled the city, very much desired a first-rate school system and actively supported efforts to create one," writes Helmreich. But "fortunate" is not the right word here. Lulled by the quality of the schools, Newark Jews only made "sporadic efforts" to set up schools of their own. Not until recently was there an all-day Hebrew school anywhere in Essex County.

With some cause, almost from the very beginning, Catholic leaders distrusted public educators, and the feeling was mutual. In the years after the Civil War, some thirty-four states passed what are called "Blaine Amendments." These amendments to state constitutions basically forbade all state aid to parochial schools. Without intending, anti-Catholic activists helped preserve the integrity of Catholic education. Catholic schools, in turn, helped preserve the viability of ethnic neighborhoods throughout America, certainly in Roseville. If I had to attend the public school on my block, we would not have moved to Myrtle Avenue. Despite massive overcrowding at St. Rose's—there were sixty-six kids in my fourth-grade class—we were still running at least a half-year ahead of Roseville Avenue School academically. Similarly, the better Catholic high schools in the area outpaced my neighborhood high school, Barringer.

The quality of students predicted the quality of the schools. For reasons both cultural and genetic, Jews long ago proved the futility of pursuing educational "equity." Starting with no more "privilege" than any other ethnic group in Newark, Jewish students consistently outperformed all others. The Berg children were a case in point. Despite systemic discrimination against Jews, especially in the Ivy League, Samuel Berg got his MD. His sister Ethel secured her teaching degrees. And brother Mo, a Barringer grad at sixteen, received his bachelor's degree from Princeton University and a law degree from Columbia University. In Roseville, this was not the norm.

As the Jewish population coalesced in Newark's Clinton Hill and Weequahic (pronounced "week-wake") sections in the 1930s and 1940s, Weequahic High emerged as arguably the top-performing public high school in America without a selective admission process. "In its halcyon days, Weequahic's students were among the best in the land," writes Helmreich. "To speak of Newark without taking note of Weequahic is impossible, for it represents much of what Newark's Jews loved about their city. They knew their school was first rate and, thus, they reasoned, so were they."

Philip Roth, Weequahic class of 1949, has made his neighborhood the most celebrated slice of literary real estate north of Faulkner's Yoknapatawpha County. "Am I wrong to think we delighted in living there?" his literary persona, Nathan Zuckerman, asks his fellow graduates in his novel *American Pastoral*. "Am I completely mistaken to think that living as well-born children in Renaissance Florence could have held a candle to growing up within aromatic range of Tabachnik's pickle barrels?"[61]

In an impressive work of urban ethnography Sherry Ortner reached out to her fellow grads in the Weequahic class of 1958 to recapture one of the final moments of Weequahic's glory, both the high school and the neighborhood. Ortner was one of 304 graduates in that class. After graduation, she proceeded to get a PhD in anthropology from the University of Chicago, won a MacArthur genius grant in 1990, and went on to teach at Columbia University among other places. For a Weequahic grad this was not exceptional. As Ortner notes, an astonishing 60 percent of the graduates from her year would "easily be described as part of America's wealthy 'white overclass.'"[62]

The fellow who recommended Ortner's book to me was one of my younger running mates from Pigtails Alley. After I lost touch with Brendan, he won a scholarship to Harvard out of a Newark public high school and enjoyed a notable career, ultimately landing a gig as Ortner's colleague at Columbia. So few people who came out of Roseville enjoyed this level of academic success, I had a hard time processing the information.

In 1958, 83 percent of Ortner's 303 classmates were Jewish. There was just a "handful" of African Americans. A sundry assortment of other ethnics, most of whom lived at the fringes of the neighborhood, rounded out the school population. In 1958, only one ethnic group had as coherent an identity as the Jews of Weequahic, and these were the Italians of North Newark. No group concerned the Jews more or intrigued them as much. Philip Roth, for instance, recounts with a shudder the "postgame pogroms" that Barringer students would inflict on the Jews of Weequahic "particularly after a rare Weequahic victory."

Jewish parents worried more about their daughters than their sons. "Dating non-Jewish persons, even white ones, was almost as strongly forbidden as dating Black persons," writes Ortner. Of all the White ethnics, she adds, "There was something of a tendency to glamorize the Italian Americans."[63] Several of her classmates admitted to a weakness in this regard. "I was just sort of fascinated by the non-Jewish kids, the Italians and the Irish, and so on," said one woman. "And I was always attracted to the guys. I don't know why, you know. I had an Italian boyfriend and my parents didn't want me to see him."

Frank, an Italian friend from Roseville, dated a few Weequahic girls and confirmed this understanding. "Got along with their families," he tells me, "but was informed not to get serious as they were going to marry nice Jewish boys." This reminds me of one of my mother's many ethnic axioms: Italians—good wives, bad husbands; Jews—good husbands, bad wives. From her perspective, if an Italian man married a Jewish woman, the couple would self-combust before the reception was over.

Understandably, Jews take pride in the their academic and economic success. Some Jews would like to think of themselves as more successful in the realm of race relations as well. Ortner insinuates as much in her account of a Black Barringer transfer she calls "William Smallwood." William's family had moved to Newark from West Virginia when he was a sophomore in high school. Upon arriving, he enrolled in Barringer.

"It was a very bad experience for me, I couldn't believe it," he tells Ortner.

Here, in an unusual move, Ortner injects herself into the conversation. "You mean there was a lot of racism at Barringer?"

Responds William, almost on cue, "Oh, my God, I couldn't believe it. I was so glad to get out of there I didn't know what to do."

Ortner suggests that the Barringer experience of Amiri Baraka poisoned his whole take on Newark. "Baraka," she writes, "holds a rather different set of feelings about Newark than Philip Roth's warm nostalgia."[64] In fact, Baraka writes almost as lovingly about his childhood as did Roth. In his autobiography, he dedicates pages to the simple joys of boyhood in his mixed-race neighborhood: "The games and sports of the playground and streets was one registration carried with us as long as we live. Our conduct, strategies, and tactics, our ranking and comradeship. Our wins and losses."[65]

Yes, Barringer was as tough as advertised. In the course of researching this book, I interviewed perhaps a score of people who went there in the 1960s, almost all Italian. They understand why Blacks might have found the environment less than accommodating. That conceded, I have to question Ortner's assumption that Barringer was "so much more overtly racist than Weequahic."

Much depends on the word "overtly." Given the scope of her book, Ortner chooses not to explore in any depth the degrees of racism among various ethnic groups. Her caution is well advised. She would need to face one reality head on. The Italians did not cut and run from Newark. The Jews did. In failing to use the word "crime" anywhere in her book, Ortner suggests her unreadiness to discuss the deeper truths about Weequahic. As shall be seen, Roth had no such reservation.

HOMESTEADING

A family photo that surfaced recently captures very close to the moment my parents became homesteaders. In the foreground of the photo are two young women dressed to the nines. The background of the photo captures the front stoop of 29 Myrtle. Sitting on the milk box in a T-shirt, his Raleighs rolled up in his shirtsleeve, is my father. Sitting on the steps, smoking a cigarette, is my mother. Neither is paying attention to the young women being photographed. They appear not to have known the girls despite them being their next-door neighbors.

The photo remains in the family for one simple reason: Ellen Hanlon, twenty at the time, would one day marry my mother's younger brother, Andy Purcell. Her sister Peggy Hanlon, then seventeen, was dressed for her high school graduation. I would place the photo in June 1955. We would have just moved from our second-floor apartment at 7 Myrtle. For my parents, this home represented a huge step into the great American middle class. Among my friends in Pigtails Alley we were the only homeowners.

According to what I read we would have been easy prey for the legendary "blockbusters." When I google the word "blockbusting" I get nearly two billion hits. The description of the phenomenon and the supporting anecdotes vary little from one study to the next. In an article on White flight in Newark, author Colleen O'Dea provides a conventional take on the subject. "As blacks moved from the South into cities like Newark," O'Dea writes, "real estate agents stoked fears that homes would lose their value, prompting whites to sell and move out." For evidence, she quotes Max Herman, a professor of sociology and anthropology at New Jersey City University, "[Real estate agents] went to neighborhoods where they encouraged a black family to move in—in some cases, even paid black women to push a baby carriage down the street to make it look like black people were moving in," Herman elaborates. "The message of blockbusters was, 'Black people are moving in, your property values are going to go down, so you'd better sell while you can.'"[66]

I don't doubt that somewhere in some city some real estate hustler hired a Black woman with a baby carriage. It is just that I have not been able to find a firsthand account of the same. Nor can I identify the city, let alone the neighborhood, in which said incident took place. Equally elusive is a confession by a repentant blockbuster or baby carriage pusher. Despite the lack of attribution, these stories are repeated endlessly. I do not trust them.

What I do know is what I saw. I can say with some confidence that blockbusting had little or nothing to do with Roseville's collapse. Like most Newark neighborhoods, ours was overwhelmingly a neighborhood of renters. It was also heavily Catholic. The quality of the public schools mattered little. People had no reason to flee. Few had a home to sell or the money to buy one elsewhere. "'Redlining' discouraged whites from moving into cities," O'Dea insists. Presuming redlining existed, it obviously did not discourage my parents from buying a house on an integrated block in Newark.

When my parents bought their home in 1954, there were already several Black families living on Myrtle. Half the students at the public school on our block were Black. Given my parents' hard-knock childhoods, these were not worrisome indicators. Homeownership trumped all other concerns. Sitting on the milk box, surveying his domain, my father had arrived.

When we moved, we did not hire movers. My father's cousin Vince, a plumber and something of a scoundrel, came by with his flatbed truck. We all pitched in to carry stuff. As reward, we boys got to ride in the open back of the truck down the block. Vince brought his "snake" down to the basement and unclogged the drains. He let me take a turn or two with it. All the other work that needed doing around the house my father did. He let us help tile the dining room ceiling, insulate the attic that would become our bedroom, and paint what needed to be painted.

Dad had other skills that seemed fully out of character with his upbringing. One was his ability to twirl a lasso. Not only could he twirl it, but he could also step in and out of it while spinning. Then, too, he could jump rope like a champ. He taught me to do both. The former never really took, but the latter did. If not the best player on my school basketball teams, I was always the best rope jumper.

Even as a kid, I sensed my father's pride in ownership. He happily stayed home with us just about every evening. No barhopping for him, no clubbing. Sitting in an easy chair in the far corner of the living room, often with my sister in his lap, he presided benignly over our TV viewing. Save for *Friday Night Fights*, he never imposed his will on what we watched. Here in his ramshackle castle on Myrtle Avenue, he was secure in a way he never was as the only child of an abandoned, crippled mother. I can imagine his response to a would-be blockbuster. "You want me to do what?"

Only on TV did women have clothes dryers. Like most moms, my mother hung our wet clothes on the line in back. So did our neighbor, Mrs. Hanlon. The clothesline served as the mothers' own social media. The women got to talking and scheming. It turned out that Ellen Hanlon was a college student, a rarity in our world. So, too, was my uncle Andy. And both were faithful Catholics. My mother was very proud of her little brother. Neither she nor her brother Bob even *went* to high school, let alone graduated. Within two years, after some serious conniving by these two neighbor women, Ellen and Andy were married.

These were good years. Ellen commuted to her college by train. She thought nothing of walking back in the evening from the train station a few blocks away on Roseville Avenue. This was a safe walk. Famed urbanist Jane Jacobs would have loved Roseville, fond as she was of neighborhoods with "an abundance of shops and services of all sorts with old houses or newer apartments above, mingled with a variety of offices."[67]

Thanks to the dogged photography of Dr. Samuel Berg, we know all the shops that Ellen would have passed on her walk back from the train station. Heading south on Roseville Avenue was a White Castle, a little jewelry shop, a Chinese laundry that I frequented only to ogle the Chinese girl who worked there, Tetta the shoemaker, and Rexall Drug on the corner. We used to bug Tetta for old shoe heels to use for hopscotch, a game we played more ruthlessly than any other males in North America.

On the west side of Roseville was the armory where kids from all the local schools mustered every Halloween before our parade through the neighborhood. We felt particularly blessed to be Catholic that night because, unlike our public school peers, we had the next day off.

Having crossed Orange Street, Ellen may well have met friends at Gruning's ice cream emporium, a teen hangout worthy of Archie and Jughead, not to mention Moe Berg. Crossing Roseville and heading west on Orange Street, Ellen would have passed the Wonder Bar, Tillman the Jeweler, Flowers by Rupp, Ratner's Confectionery, a paint store, the Tivoli cleaners, and, on the corner of Myrtle, the office of Dr. Russell Sinoway, a Jewish optometrist and, I learned, a Barringer grad.

If hungry, Ellen could have stopped at Moy Bing's, directly across Myrtle from Dr. Sinoway, or Bodholt's diner across Orange, a classic hangout. If not, she would turn left on Myrtle, walk and check in at home with her ever-watchful father. Just ten years later, Ellen would not have dared to make this walk alone.

When I posted an account of my book project on my grade school's alumni page, I learned that my affection for Roseville was universal or close to it. What follows are just a few of the responses. The first of these is wonderfully comprehensive. In its many details, it captures precisely what made the neighborhood special.

ॐ

St. Rose of Lima sat at the heart of the entire community stretching to Bloomfield Ave and Branch Brook Park. The Church and School sponsored many affairs and sponsored plays, movies, school trips on boat rides, two Drum and Bugle Corps., annual Spaghetti Supper, etc.

The community had soap box derbies, Halloween parades, ice skating rinks as well as all of the small stores lining the streets sitting amongst single family homes, apartment buildings, doctors offices, funeral homes, bus stops and the train stations. The neighborhood had everything. It was truly Idyllic.

The Church was vibrant and even had a beautiful basement Church to handle overcrowding on Sunday. It was beautifully appointed during the Holidays.

There were St. Patrick's Day parades and the old neighborhood even had a large Thanksgiving

Day parade up Roseville Ave. Throw in a couple of movie theaters and Schools Stadium to watch football games and fireworks on the 4th of July, playgrounds galore and even our own neighborhood hospital where many of us old timers were born. And let's not forget all of the deli's and the butcher shops. The Christmas decorations up and down Orange street.

CB

Any of us who grew up in Roseville in the 50's/60's experienced "idyllic" city and neighborhood life: school, churches, movies, Branch Brook park and our ice rink, The Halloween parade, playgrounds, Orange St. shopping etc. Lucky Us!

CB

We had it all, the friends, the families, the neighborhood culture, and endless days and nights of sitting on the front porch and sharing time together.

CB

I loved my childhood and I never took it for granted. I grew up in the house that my mother grew up in. She had lived there from the time she was two years old. My grandfather moved his wife and five children there to be closer to West

Orange where he worked in the Thomas Edison Laboratories.

⁂

I loved the independence I acquired by being able to safely walk or take a bus to wherever I needed to go from a young age…, I am so grateful for our community and having been able to grow up there. I am truly blessed to this day to have wonderful friendships and memories from that wonderful town and times.

Most of these commenters left Roseville as adolescents or young adults. They and their parents did not leave easily or even willingly. The notion that they panicked at the first sight of Black people is as wrongheaded as it is insulting.

⁂

Leaving Roseville was one of the hardest and most emotional parts of my life. I knew that things had changed. But in my heart, Roseville will always be my home. I will always love our house on the corner of No. 9th and 4th Ave.

⁂

We had a wonderful Childhood and didn't know it until we see the way things changed.

❧

God, I miss the Roseville Section. Leaving there was the hardest thing I've ever done. It just wasn't safe to live there anymore.

❧

Idyllic can be an overused word when thinking about our past, but I don't believe it is in our case. I've always envied those that can go home again.

I met my wife, Joan, at Purdue in the early 1970s where we both attended graduate school. When I first visited her humble hometown in western New York, I was taken aback by the very constancy of her world. Many of her friends remained in place. Others who had gone away were home for the holidays. They gathered in the same bars they had always gathered in. They ate at the same restaurants, shopped at the same shops, attended the same churches.

We stayed in the house Joan grew up in and met neighbors who had always been her neighbors. The town's daily newspaper reported on the scores of local bridge tournaments, the pink flamingos swiped from a senior's lawn, and occasionally even Joan's arrival back in town. I found myself envying Joan and all the young people across America who *could* go home again. By 1970, I and my friends from Roseville could not. There was no longer any home to go home to.

NONE OF OUR BOYS

n 1957, the year *Leave It to Beaver* debuted, I was rudely made aware that Roseville had a rougher edge to it than Beaver's "Mayfield." On one of the last days of the school year, my mother sent me to H&B's, likely for Ring Dings or Raleighs or some other essential. (If I might put in a good word for Raleighs, their coupons purchased every clock, scale, and toaster in our home.)

It was lunch time. Mom entrusted me with a five-dollar bill, a massive sum at the time, and cautioned me to be careful with the change. I should add that I never had a wallet or carried keys until I started college. Our house was never locked. Upon leaving the store, I stuck three dollar bills in my back pocket and headed home. After turning the corner of Myrtle, a pair of hands covered my eyes from behind. I was not alarmed. Kids often did this to one another, probably still do.

"Hey, Earl," I said, "what's going on?" Earl was my Black friend from the block. We bonded over the Dodgers. He forever endeared himself to me by giving me a vintage Duke Snider card that today might be worth more than my house if my mother hadn't thrown it out. Indeed, America's mothers collectively threw out enough baseball cards of sufficient current value to pay off the national debt.

Earl didn't answer. It wasn't Earl. I realized as much when another set of hands dug into my back pocket and extracted the three dollars. By the time I figured out what was going on, it was all over. I turned to see three Black kids running back down Myrtle toward Orange Street. The one kid, the tallest, was wearing a rayon shirt, all the rage at the time. That was my best clue.

I trudged home, less freaked out by the mugging than fearful of my mother's reaction when she realized I lost the money. Something of a con artist herself, Mom grilled me to make sure I had not bamboozled her out of the change. Once satisfied I was on the level, she uttered two words, one of which—"bastards"—I had never heard her use. There was no cursing allowed in my house. The other—"black"—I had not heard her use in the context of race. She completed that thought, adding, "Those Black bastards, they mugged the wrong kid."

Indeed they had. My father had recently been promoted from driving a patrol car to working as a youth aid detective in a precinct just a few blocks away. He was home within minutes. He and I walked down the block to the scene of the crime, the spot where Pigtails Alley doglegs into Myrtle, and then walked up Pigs to Roseville Avenue School, no more than fifty yards away. The principal I remember as a heavyset White woman who wore too much jewelry. She assured my father that her boys would never do such a thing. I almost laughed. Even as a nine-year-old I knew she was talking nonsense.

The principal suggested we try South Eighth Street school about a half mile away and virtually all Black. "If I am not mistaken," said my father calmly, if ironically, "you have a fair share of black boys at this school, and we're within spitting distance of the crime scene." After much huffing, the principal gave my father permission to tour the school. She didn't have much choice.

Now the burden fell on me, and I was petrified. All I had to go on was that one rayon shirt. We went from class to class, causing a stir wherever we went. Unable to spot the perp in the rayon shirt, I could sense the seeds of doubt sprouting in my father's usually trusting soul.

We were down to the last classroom. As soon as we walked in, a goofy Black kid in the front row pulled a book up in front of his face. Inferring guilt from his gesture, I pointed at the kid, "Dad, I think he's one of them."

My father said, "Son, can you come up here a second."

The kid panicked. Springing up from his seat, he blurted out, "I didn't take that boy's three dollars." In the office of the now red-faced principal, the boy promptly ratted out his co-conspirators. Crime does not always attract the best and brightest.

There is a joke philosophers tell about two logical positivists riding on a train. Upon seeing a flock of sheep, one says to the other, "There is little we can be sure of, but one thing for sure is that a flock of sheared sheep is grazing on that hillside." The other corrects him. "No," he said, "all we can be sure of us is that the sheep are sheared on the side visible from the train."

When I first heard that story, I thought of the tall boy in the rayon shirt. Upon his arrival at the principal's office, we saw that his shirt was rayon only in the back. It was quilted in the front. I was vindicated. As we were leaving the school, my father said to me in reference to the principal, "The one problem with Jews is that they think coloreds can do no wrong." It was the only time I ever heard him offer any comment about Jews. About Blacks he made no comment. He chose not to generalize beyond the one incident.

My first official mugging was quirky enough to make the *Newark Evening News*. "Dad Avenges $3 Robbery," declared the headline. The opening sentence summed up the story, "Three 11-year-old boys were arrested by the detective father of a 9-year-old boy whom the trio stopped on the street and robbed of $3 yesterday in front of 55 Myrtle Avenue." As the *Evening News* told the tale, I reported the incident to my father, "Detective William Cashill of the Youth Aid Bureau," and then we "toured the neighborhood." The three confessed and were released to their parents' custody. In retrospect, I wonder how all our lives would have been different had the one perp not given himself away. The newspaper failed to report the race of either me or the aspiring young muggers. Given our ages and the city's general calm, that fact may not have seemed relevant. In the years ahead, the more relevant that fact became, the less likely the media were to report it.

The *Newark Evening News* missed the rest of the story, which was just as well. The rumor circulated that I fought off the muggers. Liking the rumor, I said nothing to dispel it. The perps apparently wanted the record corrected. A day or two after the incident, they and a crew of their homies descended on the St. Rose playground looking for me. I had just left, but I heard plenty about their visit the next day. I decided not to tell my parents about this near miss. Going forward, I kept all such incidents to myself. There was plenty to conceal.

One other incident that summer is worth noting. My father took sick, so sick that he could not get out of bed. That never happened. He was indestructible, or so we thought. One evening I heard the sound of men rushing up the stairs. I could not see who they were as a set of curtained glass doors screened the stairs from the living room. Given the urgency of the footsteps, I knew the men were not coming for Mrs. Montgomery, our elderly boarder on the second floor. They were coming for my father. A surge of anxiety, altogether new to me, swept through me like an electric shock.

My father's appendix had ruptured. My mother shipped us out to relatives while my father flirted with death at Presbyterian Hospital a block away. Uncle Bob and Aunt Lucille took me in. They lived in a multifamily compound in a largely Italian neighborhood. Although less than two miles from our house, the neighborhood seemed to me continents away. This was a different world. The smells were different, the sounds, the shouting, the hugging.

Lucille's many relatives—mother, brother, sisters—all lived in the very same building. They welcomed me like the Prodigal Son. The mother had a homemade pizza always at the ready, and the sister, who worked for the Mars Company, had an endless bowl of M&Ms. During that stay, I learned my first Italian: "*Mangia, mangia!*"

One evening, Aunt Lucille took me to a street fair at nearby St. Rocco's Church. Thinking of my father, I decided to play the cigarette wheel. I put a dime down and on the very first turn of the wheel won a carton. "How old are you, kid?" the vendor asked me. "Nine," I answered. Telling me I was too young, he shooed me away. I went and got my aunt. Outraged, she came back with a posse of her lady friends. "He's not too young to play, just too young to win?" Her tone said it all. This guy sensed his very existence hinged on giving the right answer.

A few days later, with my father well enough to receive visitors, I went to the hospital with my carton of Raleighs in hand. My father shared a ward with probably a dozen other men. At least half of them were sitting up in bed smoking. In the absence of air-conditioning, the windows were thrown open, and multiple fans whirred noisily. If the fans made communication difficult, the construction project next door made it nearly impossible. Shouting over the jack-hammering, one of the men commented on what a good son I was for bringing my dad some cigarettes. I suspect he hoped to share in the booty. Hospitals were different then, a difference we fail to appreciate today.

Founded in 1909, Presbyterian Hospital was praised in 1912 by the Newark Board of Trade for "conducting its work without distinction as to color, nationality, or religion." I was born there. So was Whitney Houston. In that more hopeful era there was less systemic racism than academics would like to think, and they think about systemic racism a lot.

ENDANGERED SPECIES

"**A**ny analysis of architecture and planning policy that ignores the broader problems of institutional racism and economic inequality can only ever tell part of the story," writes urbanist Stefan Novakovic in an article titled "The Death of the Highrise."[68] Writing specifically of Chicago, but more broadly about all of urban America, Ta-Nehisi Coates observes, "Beginning in 1950, site selection for public housing proceeded entirely on the grounds of segregation."[69] There is nothing unusual about either observation, and there is some truth to both, but neither explains the fate of Columbus Homes.

The story that amateur historian George Langston Cook tells of growing up in this ill-fated project reveals more about its destiny and that of others like it than any academic treatise I have seen on the subject. In the way of background, Cook's family was one of the first of more than fifteen hundred original families to occupy the project when it opened in 1955 on the site of what had been Little Italy.

For Cook's family—two parents, seven kids—Columbus Homes was a midcentury wonder. He writes in loving detail of the complex's metal fire doors, fireproof walls, modern wiring, multiple playgrounds, and a construction solid enough to withstand a nuclear blast. "No home heating system I've ever encountered," he writes, "compared to the steam heat running through the project radiators during the winter."[70]

His family occupied a five-and-a-half room apartment with pastel-colored walls and buffed tile floors. Every window that opened had a screen. The small kitchen came with a gas stove and a refrigerator, both new. The boys shared one bedroom, the girls another, and the parents a third. Every other building had a laundry in its lobby. Milkmen delivered their product to the individual apartments. Bread men did the same. Doctors made house calls.

At the beginning, Italians were the project's dominant ethnic group followed by Blacks, Puerto Ricans, and other White ethnics. For the Cooks, as for most newcomers of all ethnicities, this was luxury living. They saw their existence at Columbus Homes as a privilege, one not to be taken for granted.

Almost to a person, urbanists and politicians would blame project design for the demise of Columbus Homes and other high-rises, but in the beginning, the buildings worked. "No discussion of this neighborhood could be complete," writes Cook, "without discussion of how it was kept." Again, in great detail, he describes the care that went into keeping up appearances:

> Janitors swept and mopped down every floor and stairwell daily.... Burned out lights on every floor and landing were replaced on a daily basis as well. The outside grounds were either swept or raked, papers picked up and properly disposed.... The

last thing anyone had to worry about was the cleanliness of the facility.[71]

The individual apartments were held to comparable standards. They were inspected every six months and, Cook writes approvingly, "the eviction for property damage was a real threat." Every two years, the units were completely repainted as they were whenever a tenant moved out. Without making a point of it, Cook understands why the project functioned as well as it did. "Even though Columbus Homes was public housing," he writes, "initially few poor or welfare dependent families lived there. It was first a working class neighborhood, dominated by the traditional nuclear family structure."[72] So orderly was the environment that senior citizens felt comfortable living among the families, not just in Columbus Homes but in all of Newark's high-rises. The thought was that this intergenerational exposure would be good for everyone.

When Newark's Scudder Homes first opened in 1959, the elderly, almost all Black, lived peacefully among the younger families, many of whom were related. The seniors would sit outside in the sun on cooler days or in the shade on warmer days reading, talking, smoking, playing cards or chess or dominoes, occasionally sharing stories with young relatives or friends.

Over time, the Scudder boys, like boys throughout urban America, turned wild. They amused themselves by running through the seniors' area laughing as they toppled chess boards, ripped newspapers from readers' hands, snatched hats off seniors' heads, and worse. The Housing Authority responded by fencing in the senior recreational area, but the boys quickly stepped up to the challenge. Still able to see the seniors through the chain link, they began to target them with cans, bottles, batteries, even rocks and bricks.

When I arrived in Newark in 1982, the Housing Authority had just replaced the fence with a thick concrete wall too high to see over. I talked to some of the seniors. To a person they hated the wall. It blocked the sun. That was problem enough, but what they really hated about the wall was the recognition they needed it. Amidst their own flesh and blood, they had become an endangered species, and no one of consequence cared enough to save them.

DIVIDED HIGHWAYS

Long before he became famous, comedian Joe Piscopo and his family took a ferry on a drive to Virginia. A woman spotted their New Jersey plates and exclaimed, "Hey, hey, you're from Jersey." When Piscopo answered in the affirmative, the woman asked, "What exit?"[73]

During his heyday on *Saturday Night Live*, Piscopo, in the persona of Paulie Herman of Piscataway, immortalized the question, "What exit?" Before then, no one really thought to identify himself or herself by a highway marker. Since then, I have been asked to name my exit many times. My answer, 145, in the shadow of the giant Pabst Blue Ribbon Bottle.

For the record, that exit was off the Garden State Parkway. Curiously, many media accounts of the Piscopo story suggest that people identify with their exit on the New Jersey Turnpike. They don't. Intimidating and unlovable, with limited access, the turnpike moves drivers through the diagonal length of New Jersey and out. Built in 1952 and lined with every stinking industrial facility known to man, this storied toll road has left many a passer-through wondering whether the designation "Garden State" was some kind of inside joke.

By contrast, the parkway is for ordinary New Jersey people doing ordinary things, most notably going "down the shore," a phrase that in New Jersey has long since reached the status of shibboleth. Newcomers beware: "down the shore" is one expression that bears no substitute.

For every mile I have ridden on the turnpike, I have ridden a hundred on the parkway, and my experience is, I suspect, the norm. Constructed in sections between 1946 and 1957, the parkway runs north-south from the New York State line to the southern tip at Cape May. If its primary intent was to deliver city dwellers to the shore, it quickly became a road for commuters as well.

As with many other cities in the north and east, the most attractive Newark suburbs grew up around small towns with good rail connections. Thomas Edison chose West Orange for that reason in 1880 when he built his home there. A few years later, Edison set up shop in West Orange. Both my father and grandfather worked there, commuting out from Newark. In 1920, as mentioned earlier, the Radium Luminous Material Corporation moved its shop from Newark to Orange, another more spacious suburb with good rail connections. Many of the residents of these train-centered towns commuted to high-end jobs in New York City. In time, the demand for homes in these towns priced the working classes out of the market.

I got my comeuppance in 1982 when I came back to Newark to work. Looking for a college town for my wife and daughter on a rail line, I settled on Madison, home of Drew University, about twenty-five miles west of Newark. One Saturday morning I stopped by a real estate office in Madison and asked about renting a house. "How much are you willing to pay," the agent asked.

"Oh, seven hundred and fifty dollars a month," I boasted.

She looked at me dismissively and said, "A house?" In Kansas City at the time, seven hundred and fifty dollars could have rented me Royals Stadium, well probably not, but a realistic 90 percent of the homes in the metro.

The parkway opened a whole new territory south of the established close-in towns like Madison. One instant suburb I would get to know well bore the unlovely name "Bricktown" or "Brick" for short. Named after the industrialist Joseph Brick, the town was slapped together in the scrublands west of the Jersey Shore to accommodate the demand for housing after World War II. The two uncles of my closest childhood friend, Kenny, moved to Brick in the early 1950s.

In Newark at the time there was nothing to escape. Like so many vets, these guys just wanted a home they could afford with a yard for the kids to play in and a garage for their cars. In Roseville, there were few garages and no real yards. If these guys could have afforded something better than a cookie-cutter ranch house nearly sixty miles south of Newark, they would have bought it in a heartbeat, but they couldn't. One was a bartender, the other a butcher. The trade-off was a tedious commute from Brick to "Brick City," a vintage moniker for Newark, at least until they could find work closer to home. In 1950, four thousand or so people lived in Brick. By 2000, that figure was seventy-six thousand.

In hindsight, the rationale for both the parkway and the turnpike seems compelling. The rationale for what was then called the East-West Freeway, and now I-280, eludes me to this day. The benefits it brought did not offset the havoc it wrought. Salivating over a promised "90 percent federal aid," civic leaders were as quick to sell out Roseville as they had been in 1952 when they sacrificed Little Italy.

In March 1959, the State Highway Department effectively put out a contract on Roseville's life. Those who read the "East-West Freeway study: an analysis of two alignments"—and I suspect my father was one of them—knew the neighborhood was doomed.[74] Certainly, Pigtails Alley was. So was our house. Reading the document today I am reminded of just how cavalier planners can be about destroying neighborhoods.

As proposed, the freeway was to run a little more than twenty miles from suburban Morris County in the west to the New Jersey Turnpike just east of Newark. First among the "standards" to be considered for the Newark section was whether the proposed freeway recognized the city "as the business and industrial center of New Jersey." The shiny new turnpike, a wonder of its age, should have satisfied the megalomania of civic leaders. It delivered all the commercial traffic Newark could bear right to the city's commercial door, but the movers and shakers wanted more. I suspect a few of them were eying all those federally funded demolition contracts.

Among the eight "standards" assessed in the 1959 study, the question of "how much damage" the freeway would "inflict upon residential and commercial areas through which it passes" ranked only sixth. Ranked higher were variables such as "sufficient entrances and exits in Newark" and "exit ramps for downtown."

The eighth of the eight standards asked whether the freeway would enhance "development of the area through which it passes rather than becoming a deterrent to residential and commercial development." To give the illusion of concern, planners offered up a straw man in the form of a "J alignment," an elevated road running above the neighborhood. The designers described the elevated highway in language worthy of Stephen King, so gloomy and ghastly were its likely effects.

The J alignment, planners concluded, would "permanently divide the community." After dismissing the dreaded J option, the planners countered with the seemingly more humane K alignment. This plan, which called for a depressed six-lane roadway through the very heart of a vibrant neighborhood, seemed positively benign by comparison.

The idea that planners consciously used highways to divide White and Black neighborhoods has long been gospel among the antiracist crowd. In November 2021 Transportation Secretary Pete Buttigieg said in full view of the nation what ideologues have been saying in the cozy confines of their classrooms for decades, namely that America built its highways on a bedrock of hate.

Reporter April Ryan obviously thought so. At a press conference, she asked Buttigieg in a language he seemed to understand, "Can you give us the construct of how you will deconstruct the racism that was built into the roadways?" The "racist" highway reminds me of the Black woman with the baby carriage in a transitional neighborhood. One might exist. It is just that no one bothers presenting evidence of the same.

Buttigieg felt no need to present evidence. In fact, he expressed surprise that anyone would doubt that highways were built "for the purpose of dividing a white and a black neighborhood."[75] My experience makes me wonder whether any interstate anywhere was built to divide a neighborhood along racial lines. Metro Kansas City, where I live, has more freeway miles per capita than any city in America, and not one of those miles divides a Black neighborhood from a White one. In the KC metro, as in most, more than 90 percent of the residents displaced to build the interstates were White.

In Newark, the only dividing that the East-West Freeway did was to sever the largely White northern part of Roseville from the largely White southern part. By 1959, Newark was 35 percent Black. If the designers' goal was to divide by race, they missed an easy opportunity. They missed again when, in 1963, they plotted I-78 through what were then the heavily Jewish neighborhoods of Weequahic and Clinton Hill and the predominantly White adjoining towns of Hillside and Irvington.

Newark Mayor Leo Carlin and other civic worthies approved the dissection of our neighborhood. But then again, Carlin did not live in Roseville. He and much of the city's governing elite lived in Vailsburg. That gave my mother one more reason to resent Carlin and the freeway.

My mother had something of a history with Vailsburg. In 1960, on our trip back from Florida, we pulled into a rest stop to eat a lunch she had packed before leaving Nana's. There was only one other car at the rest stop. It had New Jersey license plates, a rare sight in rural Northern Florida. Sitting at a picnic table eating was a couple roughly my parents' age.

"Hey, neighbors," the woman sang out as we disembarked. "Always good to see someone from New Jersey." Minor digression: people from New Jersey refer to their state as "New Jersey," not "Jersey." No offense, Joe Piscopo and/or Paulie Herman of Piscataway.

"Oh, hi," said my mother and wandered over to talk.

"Where are you folks from?" asked the woman.

"Newark," said my mother. "How about yourselves?"

"Vailsburg," the woman answered.

I doubt if the woman noticed, but my mother's face glaciated. I had seen the look before. Lest she betray her pique, my mother added a few more pleasantries and returned to our table, muttering under her breath, "Vailsburg!"

The ice melted but slowly. About every hundred miles or so on the way north, unprovoked and out of the blue, my mother sneered in mock snootiness, "Vailsburg!" Having seen this mood before, my father knew enough to leave it alone. So did Bob and I. My six-year-old sister, Maureen, asked, "What's Vailsburg?" and her question went unanswered. She would learn soon enough. My mother would retell the story for years to come.

Vailsburg is not another city in New Jersey. It is just another part of Newark, then slightly more Irish and middle class than Roseville, but "lace curtain" only by the most generous standards. My mother may not have read Freud, but she understood "the narcissism of small differences" well enough to be offended by its display.

If the life of any one individual highlighted the difference between the two neighborhoods, it was Big Bill Brennan's. When Bill, an Irish immigrant, worked as a coal heaver at the Ballantine Brewery, he lived in Roseville. It was there on

North 7th Street, according to the 1910 census, that his son William spent his earliest years. When Bill stopped heaving coal and started organizing coal heavers, he moved the family to Vailsburg.

In classic Irish tradition, Bill veered from union work into politics and emerged as the most powerful mover and shaker in Newark. That power helped William, a mediocre student, find his way to Harvard Law School. During the Depression, William prospered as the token Irish Catholic at Newark's leading white-shoe law firm. The increasingly affluent William settled his family in the upper-middle-class suburb of South Orange, just west of Vailsburg. This wasn't White flight. It was classic upward mobility.

William had the luck of the Irish. For political reasons, Republican Governor Alfred Driscoll appointed Brennan to the New Jersey Supreme Court in 1951. In 1956, to help secure the Catholic vote in the northeast, President Dwight Eisenhower appointed Brennan to the US Supreme Court. Justice Antonin Scalia would call the activist Brennan, who served for thirty-four years, "probably the most influential Justice of the century."[76] Scalia did not mean this as a compliment.

Among other controversial rulings, Brennan wrote the 1973 opinion for the majority in *Keyes v. School District No. 1, Denver*. The ruling mandated that Denver maintain appropriate racial balance among Whites, Blacks, and Hispanics in Denver schools. This decision did little but accelerate middle-class flight from Denver. Brennan apparently failed to anticipate that parents of all races might object to putting their little ones on buses for exhausting hours every day to solve someone else's theoretical problem.

That problem went unsolved. In 1981, Rachel Noel, the Black school board member instrumental in getting the case before the Supreme Court, admitted the plan's failure. "We have Black kids and white kids in school together today, but we really have segregation within the school building," she told the *Rocky Mountain News*, "that means it isn't working as it should or as we thought it would."[77] In 1995, a district court mercifully ended the experiment.

In the 1960s, Vailsburg's political clout may have been sufficient to spare it the wrecking ball. Roseville had no such luck. Still, the planners tried to convince others and perhaps even themselves that the freeway would do little harm. "The integrity of the community will be maintained," they insisted.

As children of the fifties, we learned how to compartmentalize our anxieties. The fear of nuclear annihilation, for instance, never went away. Our proximity to New York City put us way too close to ground zero. I felt instant relief going down the shore or to camp in western New Jersey knowing that with a fifty-mile buffer from New York, I would have at least a fighting chance at survival. With every real crisis, that anxiety would bubble to the surface and then subside when the crisis passed.

We compartmentalized the East-West Freeway as well. We knew that someday it would slice right through the center of our block, but we kids lived our lives as though that day would never come. My father had no such luxury. He had decisions to make. The most pressing was whether to maintain a house whose only future buyer would be the State Highway Department. A pragmatist, he decided not to keep it up, at least not in any meaningful way. He loved the house, loved being a homeowner, and he had the skill to make the home something special. But protest was in vain. Those federal dollars spoke a whole lot louder than all the Dads of Roseville ever could.

FALL OF ROME

Between 1960 and 1980, Newark lost more than 150,000 White residents. During that same period Detroit and Chicago each lost close to a million, the great majority of whom were ethnic and working class. The pattern repeated itself in every industrial city in the northeast and north central United States. With an outward flow of multiple millions, academic researchers should have spoken with the dispossessed if for no other reason than to gauge the political impact of their departure. With rare exception, they haven't bothered.

The politics of Roseville shifted dramatically in 1960, starting with my own household. My parents, who both voted for Dwight Eisenhower in 1956, threw in with John F. Kennedy. As a twelve-year-old paperboy who consumed his own product, I was even more ardent than they in my affection. For us, as Irish Catholics, our attachment to JFK was purely tribal. On policy issues, I was twelve. What did I know? Everyone I knew was for Kennedy. I still recall how pleased I felt to see some of my Italian friends parading around the neighborhood with Kennedy signs. Blacks were all in as well.

I followed the primary campaign even more intensely than I did the 1960 pennant race. Fortunately for Kennedy, he did better that year than the Dodgers. In November, he carried New Jersey with a victory margin of less than 1 percent, and it was the citizens of Newark who put him over the top. In 1956, Essex County, where we lived, went 60–37 for Eisenhower. In 1960 Essex went 55–42 for Kennedy. Kennedy did not win despite being Catholic. He won because he was Catholic.

The great ethnic diaspora reshaped party alignments. Although I did not ask about politics, many of the people with whom I spoke volunteered their opinions. Quips Phyllis, who grew up across the street from me, "Everyone from Newark ends up a Republican." In her close group of St. Rose alumni, she counts two Democrats out of "dozens." Phyllis went on to become the Republican mayor of an exurban town thirty miles from Newark.

On the other hand, Ellen, who lived directly across Pigtails Alley from me, went on to become mayor of a hip, liberal suburb adjacent to Newark. One critical difference between the two women is *when* they lived where they lived. Phyllis is six years younger than I, Ellen six years older. If Kennedy had lived until 1964, Ellen could have voted for him. Her identity as a Democrat was forged before the neighborhood got dangerous. The same dynamic holds for my former neighbor, Aunt Ellen, who remains a Democrat to this day. Thirteen years older than I, Ellen came of age in a more innocent era. She never got mugged.

Hank did. A classmate at St. Rose, I lost complete touch with him until I started this project. As he told me, he left Roseville in 1959 after the sixth grade. When I asked why, he said matter-of-factly, "Someone punched me in the face and stole my scout dues." Most Newarkers do not bother detailing the race of that "someone." It is understood. I asked anyhow just to clarify. Hank confirmed the guy was Black. He even knew his name. Apparently, the fellow had liberated the dues from several other Scouts.

Bullying and fighting were commonplace in a rough-and-tumble city like Newark. Muggings and robberies were new and unwelcome. In our neighborhood, they almost always had a racial cast to them. It was said a century or two ago that the farther you lived from the frontier, the more sympathetic you were to the plight of American Indians. A comparable sentiment was at play in America's cities. White people comfortably ensconced in the suburbs or in elite urban enclaves had little sympathy for the working-class ethnics left behind to confront the rising tide of crime.

Watching from Brentwood, California, television producer Norman Lear had less sympathy than most. In his often funny but always patronizing hit 1970s sitcom, *All in the Family*, Lear presented White fear of Black crime as little more than racist paranoia. In searching through a library of scripts, I found two episodes in which the show's central figure, Archie Bunker, is involved in a mugging, one as a victim, one as a witness. In both cases, the mugger is White. In "Archie Sees a Mugging," the mugger is described as "a long-haired blond kid." Far from Archie's Queens or other urban hot spots, that scenario might have seemed likely. In Newark, that scenario struck viewers like my mother as laughable—"Yeah, right, long-haired blond kid!"

Philip Roth had a firmer grip on reality than Lear. Nathan Zuckerman, Philip Roth's thinly disguised literary persona, is reminded of his own airy elitism in Roth's 1981 novel, *Zuckerman Unbound*. A successful author by the mid-1960s, Zuckerman has been watching Newark's implosion from his pricy digs on Manhattan's Upper East Side. One day, while out walking, Zuckerman runs smack into Alvin Pepler, a deranged fan from Newark.

"You got out in '49, right? Well, it's a different city today. You wouldn't recognize it. You wouldn't want to," Pepler tells Zuckerman, the sense of menace increasing with each exchange. "Me, I'm still over there pounding away." When Zuckerman tries to blow Pepler off, Pepler turns hostile. He calls out Zuckerman for his elitism and ignorance, his failure to acknowledge the "barbarian hordes and the Fall of Rome!"

"What do you know about Newark, Mama's Boy! I read that fucking book," Pepler scolds Zuckerman. "To you it's being Leni-Lenape Indians at school in the play! To you it's Uncle Max in his undershirt, watering the radishes at night. And Nick Etten at first for the Bears. Nick Etten! Moron! Moron!" Pepler then tells Zuckerman what Newark looks like from the perspective of those left behind:

> Newark is a nigger with a knife! Newark is a whore with the syph! Newark is junkies shitting in your hallway and everything burned to the ground! Newark is dago vigilantes hunting jigs with tire irons! Newark is bankruptcy! Newark is ashes! Newark is rubble and filth.[78]

For Hank's father, the city had become untenable before the rest of us took note. Although Hank enjoyed Roseville immensely, especially the freedom of movement it afforded him, the family moved to the suburbs. There they lived in a duplex owned by Hank's grandmother. His parents could not afford to buy a home of their own. "We must have been dirt poor," said Hank, "but I never knew it."

Roger, my good friend from Pigs, left in 1959 as well. He had been living with his father and brother in a jury-rigged, six-unit building on Roseville Avenue owned by his grandmother, a Hungarian immigrant. Shortly before Roger left Newark, he had accompanied me one afternoon on my paper route. While I ran the papers up the stairs of an apartment building, Roger waited in the vestibule. On coming back down, I saw three older Black guys encircling an uneasy Roger. As I walked in, one of the three thrust a rifle in my back and demanded my money. He tapped a dry well. All I had was a nickel. Roger had less than that. Disgusted, the gunman let me keep my nickel, and he and his buddies took off. I did not get a good look at the gun. I suspect it was an air rifle, but times were changing. Who knows? On this occasion I chose not to tell my parents. The fear of reprisal outweighed any hunger for justice.

I had thought this incident might have prompted Roger's departure, but, as I learned, he didn't tell his father either. Being in the White minority at Roseville Avenue School, he had long ago learned to keep his mouth shut. No, it was his mother's recent death that prompted the family's move forty-five miles south to Long Branch, a shore town well past its prime. Although Roger and I had been close, we had no good way of staying in contact. Back then, only a birth or death justified a long-distance call, and it was beneath our male dignity to send letters. Roger was as lost to me as if his family had moved back to Hungary.

That same year Roger left, Kenny moved into the neighborhood. We met in our sixth-grade class at St. Rose. That very first year, he became the subject of my all-time favorite Catholic school story and the only one I will tell in this book. For some reason, Sister Agnes Lucy felt it helpful to have a cow drawn on the blackboard. When she asked if there was an artist in the class, everyone pointed to Kenny. He gladly accepted the commission.

Living up to his reputation, Kenny drew a shockingly good likeness of a cow. The drawing complete, he stepped back from the blackboard, assessed his handiwork, and then, with a mischievous glint in his eyes, drew in the udder. Seeing this, a furious Sister Agnes Lucy rushed up from the back of the class and promptly slapped Kenny in the face. People tend to react in horror when I tell this story, but the good Sister did not slap Kenny for drawing in the udder. She slapped him for the mischievous glint that preceded the drawing of the udder. At the time we all understood this, Kenny especially.

The neighborhood's demise would in time lead to a Stanley-Livingstone kind of meeting between Roger and Kenny. Given the price of close-in suburban real estate, many of our friends and neighbors headed over the bridge across the Raritan and settled far from what had been home, Kenny's family among them. Six years after Roger's departure, he and

Kenny would find themselves jumping center for their respective high schools in a game fifty or so miles south of Newark. One night soon after that game, Roger showed up unexpectedly at our home on Myrtle. I had not seen or heard from him in five years. He brought a photo of that encounter with Kenny lifted from a Shore newspaper. Kenny and I would not see Roger again for fifty-five years.

AMBUSH AT THE
NEW YORK TIMES

Leah Boustan, a professor of economics at Princeton University, is something of an authority on White flight. If confirmation were needed, her book, *Competition in the Promised Land: Black Migrants in Northern Cities and Labor Markets*, won her a share of the 2018 Allan Sharlin Memorial Award presented by the Social Science History Association.

In 2017, Boustan wrote an op-ed for the *New York Times* titled, "The Culprits Behind White Flight."[79] Given the trauma of the 2016 presidential election, Boustan begins by imagining a scenario in which Democratic strategists ask themselves the question, "Was Donald Trump's surprise victory due to his voters' racism or their economic anxiety?" Her own research into post-war White flight, she explains, began with "a similar question of whodunit." The two questions, she continues, likely had the same answer. A mix of racism *and* economics led both to Trump's victory and to White flight, one outcome as unfortunate as the other.

Now here is where the op-ed gets amusing. "To complicate the picture," Boustan writes of the displaced Whites, "few of them left personal accounts, and they may not have been able to articulate exactly why they moved." I laughed out loud upon reading this. If classism were as taboo as racism at Princeton, Boustan would have been busted down to janitress. Everyone with whom I spoke knew exactly why they left. It's just that no one bothered to ask them.

Filled with meaningless statistics and observations impossible to summarize, Boustan's op-ed does not begin to answer the questions she posed. To her credit, however, she avoids the empty-headed slanders of the antiracist cartel and offers a relatively nuanced account of a complex phenomenon. "We are left reconstructing the pieces through careful detective work," she writes in conclusion. "In my own work, I have found that Poirot is often right: Each suspect wielded his own knife."

Although Boustan's metaphor has merit, in practice she models her approach less on Poirot than on another fictional Frenchman. Like the wily Captain Renault in *Casablanca*, she rounds up the usual suspects and lets the real culprits walk away. I wasn't the only one who noticed. As one reader observed in the comment section, "I suppose I should be used to it by now, but I still find it kind of astonishing to read an analysis of white flight which doesn't even mention the word 'crime.'"

I confess to having read the comment section to see whether readers hammered Boustan for being relatively soft on fleeing Whites. Some, of course, did. Several faulted her for paying too little heed to the gospel of blockbusting. One nervy reader felt the need to explain the conspiracy to Boustan as though it were something she had never heard before:

Real estate agents were commissioned to sell property in the suburbs so they created blockbusting—
they'd sell one house to a black family and then
frighten the white neighbors into selling out and
buying the houses they offered in suburbia.

The reader clarified that for these "working class homeowners" their house was their biggest asset. Again, I cannot
speak for all neighborhoods everywhere, but among my many
friends from Pigtails Alley, we were the only ones with a home
of our own, and we bought into our block *after* several Black
families had moved in. Newark, for the most part, was a city
of renters. As I saw in my recent tour of Newark, however, at
least a few of the neighborhoods with high homeownership
rates had yet to flip. Where's Poirot when we need him?

I confess to misjudging the readers of the *Times*. To my
great surprise, many of them showed a keener understanding of White flight than Boustan. Scores of these readers
from across the country shared their personal stories. Contra
Boustan, all were able to articulate exactly why they moved. A
dozen of these narratives follow. Most identified the city they
fled. The emphasis is added, but the text is copied as was:

ভ

We tried to stick it out—my parents wanted to
spend money on our college educations, not a new
house—but the neighborhood, where a ten year
old could walk home 5 blocks from synagogue at
8 at night, overnight became a place where white

kids…would have their bus and lunch money robbed from them. Ta-Nehisi Coates has no idea what he is talking about. By the time we left the East Mt Airy section of **Philadelphia** in 1970 the first black families who had moved in were getting out too.

◌ଃ

I grew up in a modest lower middle class neighborhood on the near-eastside of **Detroit**. We never considered it a ghetto. After the late 1960's we saw a surge of Black Power and also [a]n increase in crime an racial violence. Many of us were Democratic Party supporters. When we sought some sort of relief from the crime we were accused of being "afraid of the unknown." As crime became worse many folks moved out, and they were accused by liberals of "not wanting to share power"…. Finally one evening our telephone lines were cut and I chased would be assailants away with a firearm. We moved out soon afterwards then came the chorus: "See, white flight, that's the reason we're a ghetto now!"

◌ଃ

I left **New Haven** because I gained the distinct impression that city government considered me a cow to be milked for tax money. They emphatically did not care about my concerns. When my mother-in-law was assaulted, knocked to the ground and had her purse stolen, there was no investigation, barely an expression of concern or sympathy. When I was robbed at the train station, the perp escaped into the nearby public housing, and that was the end of it. The city's entire focus was providing services to people other than me or those like me. When a teacher was murdered at the high school, that sealed the deal.

03

My grandmother refused to leave her home in inner city **Detroit**. My aunt and family lived upstairs; after my cousin was mugged on her way to Catholic school they moved out, leaving my grandmother. Her home was broken into multiple times; the neighborhood grocery left due to crime. After she died, her 2 family brick home, lovingly cared for, resided in a slovenly mess of a neighborhood. It sold for less than $10,000, an unfortunate lesson to her working class children.

03

My dear departed mother was a NYC fifth grade teacher in **Queens** and we all attended the fine local grade school containing a mix of students. She moved us to a town in NJ, known for its excellent school system and where she intended to teach, just prior to my oldest sister attending the large centralized area high school. She had inside knowledge of the violence, disruptive students and lower quality of education at the 50% black high school. Mom was no racist, devoted to her many black and foreign students, but desired a top notch educational environment for her children.

CB

After my grandfather died my grandmother was left alone in their house and the house next door sold to a minority "family". My grandmother had lived in that house 50+ years and had never had a bad encounter with any neighbor in that next door row house. That changed instantly with the arrival of her new neighbor. All night partying, drinking, uninterested and absent parents leading to out of control children, trash in the yard, frequent visits by law enforcement, a "father" who seldom if ever worked, never mowing their grass, or shoveling snow off the sidewalk, etc. When she finally confronted them about their behavior, the son threatened her. Threatened to harm a 70-some old lady. We moved her out as soon as we could, to the suburbs.

CB

It was physical fear and a desire to send one's children to functioning schools. That's why we live in Clayton, Mo., not the city of **St. Louis**, a mile away. Don't call people "racist" because they want to educate their children and don't want to be repeatedly robbed at knife or gun point, or worse. That's what elected Trump—the feeling that the Democrats (and to some extent the Republicans) don't care about ordinary people and their children, and call them racist if they act to protect themselves. I grew up in fear on the streets of New York City, and swore I would not subject my children to that.

ぐ

When the neighborhood started to become less white, we had a conversation about it, determining that no matter the color of their skin, [my mother's] neighbors wanted the same things she did. She stayed. Until the house was robbed a couple of times when she was at the grocery store. Then the neighbor two doors down was immediately shot and killed when he answered his doorbell one evening. My mother knew the man fairly well. He, too, was retired—and happened to be black. That was the sign. She moved and sold the house at a loss.

ぐ

At roughly the same time [1970s], a heroin epidemic was taking hold in the city [New York]. Street crime boomed and took an enormous toll on the quality of life in the mainland borough [**the Bronx**]. My early years were spent in a safe, working-class neighborhood. My high school and college years (I commuted) were spent in a poor, crime-ridden area in which my mother, sisters, and neighbors became routine victims. We never wanted to leave. My parents didn't drive. They appreciated that the 4 and the D took them almost everywhere. Eventually they moved to an apartment in West Yonkers. Dad's health problems may have been exacerbated by a commute that went from a ride on the 4 to two buses and three trains. He died a little more than year after the move.

 C3

How do you have an article like this without mentioning forced busing to schools in the '70s? My childhood home in **Rochester, NY** was right next store [*sic*] to the elementary school I should have attended. Not with busing—I was shipped about 5 miles away to better segregate the schools. Busing was a failure and it drove a new wave of white flight from the city. Buying or renting a house near a school you would like to have your kids attend and then having them forced to go elsewhere was unacceptable to most people.

C3

I moved into **Detroit** in the late 70s; rent was much cheaper and I liked Detroit. I was robbed the first year by my neighbors. Neighbors that routinely wrecked my garden, broke my large stones that lined the garden, and when I challenged the adults in the house, the door was slammed in my face. I was laughed at when I tried to talk to other neighbors. I'm white, they were all black. I called the police, they laughed.... Not white flight—common sense tells you to move.

∞

My family had a house in **Compton, Calif** in the 50's when the town was primarily, white, lower income. As blacks migrated in, most whites left during the 60's and 70's. We had a cute small house, and were low income. So we stayed. Most of us were poor, so no-one knew they were poor. Initially, it was fine, but as the economy worsened, the Watts riots occurred, businesses moved out, and it became hopeless, violent and dangerous. My brother was beaten daily, we were threatened that our home would be burned down, kids were knifed at school, girls hair set on fire. Gangs and drugs reigned. We eventually left for a white trailer park, on the periphery of a middle class white neighborhood. It was a relief to walk the streets and not fear getting jumped, beat, robbed.

Reading these accounts, from *New York Times* readers no less, Boustan had to feel a little foolish. These people were "able to articulate exactly why they moved." Brother beaten, girl's hair set on fire, neighbor shot, grandmother threatened—the imagery is precise, and it comes from experience, an experience about which Boustan seems oblivious. Several readers made note of Boustan's Ivy League remove from real people and real problems.

"Ms. Boustan," writes one reader, "you are a Princeton professor, supposedly capable of independent thought and analysis, please don't be so easily pulled into narrow minded, short sighted political rhetoric."

"Tellingly, this piece makes absolutely no mention of concerns for safety and the desire natural to all people to live apart from crime," writes another. "And I understand why it does not—addressing crime and its impact on where we choose to live does not fit in with any narrative that is socially acceptable for a professor of economics at Princeton to present in the pages of the NY Times."

A third reader brings the issue home. "I see that the author studied/worked at Princeton, Harvard & UCLA, all located in exclusive areas that are primarily white," he observes. "So if she is claiming to be an expert on white flight, I wonder…has she actually LIVED somewhere deeply impacted by white flight?"

During the summer of 1982, my wife, daughter, and I lived in Princeton. Each morning I boarded the express train to Newark, leaving behind America's most idyllic community and arriving just thirty-three minutes later in its most hellish. This is a journey I would recommend to all Princeton professors.

THE LAST HURRAH

During my research on this project, I came across my eighth-grade autograph book. Although class size had thinned a little since fourth grade, it still hovered around fifty.

Despite the overabundance of students, kids learned. Norman, who had been in my class since kindergarten, wrote the following without error: "In the golden chain of friendship regard me as a link." Norman's mental shortfalls were conspicuous. In a public school, he would have been consigned to special ed, and even there kids would have taunted him. Norman did have, however, a loving, protective father who worked with the nuns to get his son through school. Last I heard, Norman was a mailman.

Another surprise was Paul, an off-the-boat Puerto Rican who lived in the funky apartments at the top of Myrtle Avenue. When he arrived in the seventh grade, he could barely speak English. By the eighth grade, he was able to write, with impressive penmanship, "When you die everything will be good. When your living everything will be...." Okay, he got "your" wrong, but so would most eighth graders.

Under "class leaders" I designated my good friend Albert as both "wittiest" and "most cheerful." We had been together since kindergarten. In the fourth grade, on "bring a new kid" day, I brought Albert to my Cub Scout meeting. He was our first Black scout and among its most decorated. By the eighth grade, he had come to think of himself as the Jackie Robinson of Cub Pack 115. As my autograph book attests, ethnicity had become a subject of humor. At least three boys wrote some variation of the following:

> They're as skinny as a toothpick
> Or as fat as a cow
> If I was an Irishman
> I would end it all now

Of the three, one was Albert. Another signed off as a "big fat guinea." An Irish friend countered with:

> Roses are red
> Violets are Blue
> I ain't a guinea
> And neither are you

"The past is a foreign country," writes L. P. Hartley in his 1953 novel *The Go-Between*, "they do things differently there." That we did. When it came to exchanging barbs with other ethnic groups, we recognized few limits. Had there been a social media to capture our comments, none of us could ever have run for office, let alone hosted the Oscars. Although our language would shock our descendants, we were growing more inclusive, not less. If our progress had continued, we could have one day told jokes about Blacks to Blacks, and they would have told White jokes right back.

Our parents played by different rules. I was reminded of this on a long rainy drive to Yankee Stadium when I was about ten. My father and a police friend were in the front seat. The friend's son, my brother Bob, and I were in the back. Everyone was miserable. Driving to the Bronx is ordeal enough, but driving in a downpour, suspecting the game will be rained out (it was), depressed us all, even my usually unflappable father. From the backseat, to lighten the mood, I volunteered a joke. "Dad," I said, "why did God make the world round?"

Said my father, "I don't know. Why did God make the world round?"

Ethnic jokes work, I should explain, only when they tap a fundamental truth. For me, Polish jokes did not work for the simple reason that all the Poles I knew were pretty smart. On the other hand, the joke that begins, "What's an Irish seven-course meal," and ends, "a six-pack and a boiled potato," does work. It taps a fundamental truth.

Italians had their own quirks. In our world, their young men tended to hang out on street corners. The guys that hung out at Myrtle and Orange—a few years older than the Pigs gang—wore jackets with dice on their backs and called themselves the "7-11s." They pitched dimes, harassed passers-by, and worked on their doo-wop.

"God made the world round," I said, laughing as I answered, "to keep the Guineas off the corners." Ethnic jokes work better, I should add, when you don't embarrass your unsuspecting Dad in front of his Italian friend. When only Bob laughed with me—and he stopped quickly—I knew I had screwed up. The trip got longer still.

In the year that followed my grade-school graduation, Irish-Italian humor took a hiatus. The upcoming mayoral election would be the last in Newark to pit an Irish candidate against an Italian, and it would have ramifications for my family that we never imagined. The same winds of change that swept Kennedy into office were soon to sweep Newark's incumbent Irish mayor out.

An old school pol, Leo P. Carlin was about to experience his last hurrah. Born in Newark in 1908, one of twenty-two children, he never did graduate from high school. He didn't need a degree to work as a union organizer. His union work led to a scat on Newark's City Commission. From that position, he led the successful drive to end the commission structure and introduce a strong mayor form of government. The people of Newark elected him mayor in 1954 and again in 1958, the second time with 64 percent of the vote.

Other than in the looks department, Rep. Hugh Addonizio, a seven-term congressman, matched up well against Kennedy: college football star, war hero, liberal Democrat, youthful vigor. Importantly for "Hughie," he had something Kennedy did not, namely an Irish wife. He needed more than that to sway the old school Micks. "In every Irish parade or hall, you saw nothing but Carlin signs," said one ancient politico, "and all over the city, you could see Addonizio banners. It was really something to watch in those days—like something you see in the movies with Spencer Tracy—that type of politics."[80]

Despite their Irish roots, my parents liked Addonizio. Among other reasons, he was the benefactor of Troop 40, the Boy Scout troop that served the White remnant left behind in our old West Market Street neighborhood. Bob and I were members because Billy once was. Some months before the election in 1962, Addonizio gave nine of us our Eagle Scout awards. The photo accompanying the news story is a classic. With our studied scowls and slicked-back hair, we looked more like a street gang than a Scout troop.

My parents had a more substantial reason to back Addonizio. Although they had yet to lose their home, they held Carlin to account for the demolition to come. They were not alone. "The view of most civic groups was that Mayor Carlin was responsible for the disruptive redevelopment plans," writes scholar and civil rights activist Robert Curvin in his useful book on Newark politics, *Inside Newark*.[81]

Carlin's luck ran bad that election season. A crippling snowstorm found him in Florida, never a good place for a mayor to be when your city is paralyzed. A second disaster was of Carlin's own making. During a campaign debate, an audience member asked whether he had concerns about his opponent's integrity. If the question was a setup, it was a good one. Carlin took the bait. He responded that voters should be concerned about Addonizio's associations, adding, "Beware the Black Hand." In Newark no one needed to be told that the "Black Hand" referred to a turn-of-the-century Italian extortion ring.

Primed for the moment, an indignant Addonizio leaped out of his seat. "Are you accusing me of being tied to the Mafia?" he asked. "Are you making such accusations because I am an Italian American?"

As Addonizio's Irish campaign manager would later acknowledge, "We pounced on it…it just riled up the Italians in Newark, the biggest voting bloc in the North Ward."[82] After this blunder, Carlin never had a chance. Addonizio walked away with 62 percent of the vote.

In the election of 1962, despite continuing population loss in the city, 19 percent more votes were cast than in 1958. Addonizio's people did not need to cheat to win, but they probably did anyhow. Election fraud is a cottage industry in Newark.

I have no inside knowledge about 1962, but in 1982 I found myself with a ringside seat on a bruising battle for the mayor's chair. I had just started work at the thousand-employee Newark Housing and Redevelopment Authority. I was hired as the special assistant to the executive director, an elusive title for a concocted job. I had two qualifications that endeared me to the Philippine-born woman who ran the show: my family lived in Newark public housing after we were forced out of Roseville, and I aced her borderline illegal IQ test. An elitist whose role model was the then little-known Imelda Marcos, my "Imelda" took me under her wing.

Ignoring all election laws, Imelda and her figurehead boss—a Black "judge" of some sort—threw the whole weight of the Housing Authority behind the incumbent mayor, Ken Gibson, a political ally of the judge. Like all the other senior staff, I was expected to pony up. I wrote in my journal, the only one I ever kept, "Am told that it would be useful were I to support Gibson. 'Not perfect' according to Imelda, but she believes him to be best for city." I told Imelda I would oblige, but only if I could see how the political wheels turned. She agreed.

"Not perfect" failed to do Gibson justice. A year before my arrival, a federal prosecutor sought to indict him on tax fraud. According to the *New York Times*, he had allegedly taken money from his 1974 campaign fund and secreted "more than $75,000 in a Swiss bank account."[83] The Department of Justice would not allow the charges to be brought. Rumor had it that Jimmy Carter himself quashed the indictment.

By 1982, as Gibson sought his fourth term, Blacks dominated city politics. Gibson's chief opponent was Black City Council president Earl Harris. Italians still wielded power, but it was largely behind the scenes. On March 31 of that year, about six weeks before the May election, a special Essex County grand jury indicted both Gibson and Harris for arranging a no-show job for an old Italian politico. No one expressed shock or even surprise. This was Newark after all.

Imelda ran the agency's election effort. Sticking around after work each day and on Saturdays to finish my PhD dissertation, I watched as her mostly foreign-born staffers manned the agency's phones. They were reminding the thirty thousand or so people who lived in the projects why it was in their best interest to reelect the mayor. Imelda's staff also identified tenants of influence and made sure they got new refrigerators or even new apartments. And Imelda personally strong-armed senior staff, me included, to buy tickets for fundraisers of all sorts. Wanting to see how things worked, I attended the events. Some sample journal entries:

3-17: BB stops by to tell me I should attend reception at Thomm's Restaurant for Gibson—purpose is to assess support within Housing for mayor. Very cynical, expedient process, but everyone participates.

3-31: Talk with DL about working for Gibson. "Do I have a choice?"

4-2: "I am now indicted." First line of Gibson's speech. Says that he did nothing he wouldn't do again.

4-6: Group of people working with computer lists, turns out to be for election.

4-14: Given election sign-up sheet. Choice of days to volunteer. Must tell whether we are going to use vacation time or personal leave time.

4-26: Large crews of housing workers rounded up to canvass voters.

5-6: Resist pressure for more election work with variety of excuses.... Crews to work through weekend.

5-7: [Imelda] starts reaming me for skipping out. I explain my position. I'm not interested in Gibson. I don't want to campaign. I don't care to do it merely to keep my job.

> 7-16: Condition of [judge] keeping job, I suspect, is to purchase 250 $100 tickets for KG's campaign fund.

Sometime that spring I learned that I had been awarded a Fulbright to teach for a year at a French university, starting in September. Now with a graceful exit assured, I could really start having fun with these people. As the May 11 election approached, Imelda informed the staff, hundreds of us, that we were expected to volunteer a vacation day to help get out the vote on Election Day. Playing along, I was assigned with old-timers Joe and Sal to the senior projects in the Italian North Newark where my grandmother lived. Our job was to go door-to-door and escort the little old ladies to the polls, reminding them that if they wanted to keep their apartments, it would pay to vote for Gibson.

We never left the local coffee shop. These guys had great stories to tell about past elections and all day to tell them. The best stories were about the 1970 election, the election in which Gibson ousted Addonizio. Pointing to the polling site across the street, Joe said, "I voted there six times that day. I was dead people. I was old people. I was all kinds of people. And don't think they weren't doing the same thing on the other side of town." I took him at his word and asked him to pass the cannolis.

After my day near the polls, if not exactly at them, I headed back to the office and spoke to my young Black secretary. She was sporting a Gibson pin as big as her head. "Our man gonna win?" I asked.

"Don't matter who win," she answered. "Both them n*****s goin' to jail anyhow." What she feared most, what everyone feared, was that no candidate would get a majority of the vote. None did, which meant a runoff between Gibson and Harris and another vacation day squandered at the polls.

No longer trusting me to man the polls, Imelda assigned me to deliver fried chicken to the "volunteer" poll workers for the runoff vote. I countered by scheduling a knee operation for that same day. Imelda appreciated the moxie of my gambit.

Despite my absence, Gibson prevailed. A month later Imelda called the senior staff into a conference room in flights of about eight. She told my group, as she told the others, that to retire his campaign debt Mayor Gibson was inviting all of us to a victory breakfast. Knowing what that meant, most of the staffers pulled out their checkbooks. The only thing that surprised them was the amount—$250 or about $750 by current standards.

Imelda went around the room one by one and requested the check. "Is this mandatory?" one fellow asked timidly.

"Only if you're interested in job security," she smirked.

When she came to me, I dutifully pulled out my checkbook, smiled, and said, "Should I make the check payable in Swiss francs?" The room froze. Then Imelda laughed, and the whole room laughed with her. In Newark, everything was funny, especially elections.

POLITICAL CONSIDERATIONS

Elections, as they say, do have consequences. Carlin's "Black Hand" slur hit close to dead center. Right after the election, Hughie appointed Dominick Spina, a police inspector, to head up the Newark Police Department. When FBI tapes were made public during a later trial, Tony Boy Boiardo and co-conspirator Angelo "Gyp" DeCarlo were heard agreeing that Spina was the right guy for the job. At one point, DeCarlo tells Boiardo, "It's your call."[84]

Spina served as the new mayor's hatchet man. Although my father stayed out of politics, his captain—"Murphy" by name—had not. For Addonizio, it was payback time. By 1962, my father had received successive merit raises in his promotion to the rank of detective first grade. Under Police Director Joseph Weldon, such promotions were merit based. Each morning, Monday to Friday, Dad walked to a precinct three blocks from the house in a coat and tie. He had achieved a level of respect and respectability that he likely never anticipated in his Dickensian childhood. Within months of the election, all that was stripped away.

In 1965, at a grand jury hearing over a gambling raid gone bad, Spina conceded that he was the one who "makes the decisions regarding the transfer of personnel." He admitted, too, that he used his own standards, "particularly in regard to the rank of plainclothesmen and detective." The mayor, to be sure, often intervened in the process. Said the grand jury in a presentment: "Political considerations seem to override all else in the assignment of officers to plainclothes and gambling details."[85]

Recounting my father's career, a subsequent newspaper story read, "He recently transferred from the Youth Aid Bureau to the First Precinct."[86] The word "transferred" suggests a parallel move, possibly at my father's request. The editors apparently did not want to dig too deeply. They failed to mention that my father's new hours were midnight to 8 a.m., that his new assignment was to man the station's front desk, that he had to wear a uniform, and that he had to take a bus downtown and back so that my mother could use the car in the morning to get to her job as a school crossing guard. No one volunteers for this kind of transfer. My father was collateral damage in an ethnic war ginned up for political reasons among peoples who had long since become allies.

The newspapers did mention, "Cashill's invalid mother, Mrs. Marie Cashill, and her sister, Mrs. Elizabeth Smart," as having been in another bedroom on the second floor. There is more to this story, of course. A year before the election, Gramps died in Florida. In that era, certainly among the working class, adult children took care of their dependent parents. In the personal stories I reviewed for this book, I could see that the "grandmother" often factored into a family's decision to stay in the neighborhood or leave.

My father's "Aunt Lil," Nana's older sister, came as part of the package. Nana could not have lived without Lil's round-the-clock care, but good God did these two women despise each other. Confined to a single room, the sisters sat in opposite corners and hurled the most vile—and creative—imprecations back and forth all day long. If these ladies played the dozens, the cleverest Black kid in Newark would have had a hard time hanging in with them.

That first year they lived with us, *What Ever Happened to Baby Jane?* came to our neighborhood theater. The movie, starring Bette Davis and Joan Crawford, struck home. The plot summary read as follows, "A former child star torments her paraplegic sister in their decaying Hollywood mansion." In our decaying, soon-to-be-demolished house, the wheelchair-bound Nana did most of the tormenting. Bernie had clearly paid his dues taking care of this unhappy lady.

Even if Nana had been the Blessed Mother, her presence would have caused problems. My parents had to give up their bedroom and sleep on a foldout couch in the living room. Sixty years later, there is still not a comfortable such contraption. Patient soul that he was, my father would have endured a querulous mother-in-law. My mother did not have that patience. In Irish households, angry women do not shout. They simmer. The boil was low enough we didn't really notice. My father did. In years past, he might have found escape in painting the house or finishing the basement, but the Highway Department had rendered such efforts futile.

On the afternoon of January 6, 1963, a Sunday, my father took the Christmas tree down as he always did on the Epiphany and retreated upstairs to the small bedroom my brother Billy had just vacated upon getting married. Sometime later, my mother came home from the movies, her retreat, and headed upstairs. My brother and I were watching *The College Bowl*, one of us screaming out the answers before the other could. I had just turned fifteen, Bob sixteen. Nine-year-old Maureen was just waiting for the show to end so we would shut up, and she could watch *Lassie*.

When I first saw the hint of a strobe from up the street, I thought, *Oh, cool. Some excitement*. Then the whoops stopped in front of our house, and the strobe pierced directly into the living room. The thunder of male footsteps on the stairs leading up to the second floor completed the equation. "It must be Nana," said Bob anxiously.

I shook my head. "No," I said. "It's Dad." There was no mistaking the urgency. The cops had come for one of their own.

My brother Bob had to make the phone calls to our brother Billy, our uncle Bob, a Newark cop, and then my uncle Andy, who had moved with wife Ellen to suburban Cedar Grove months before. "Get down here right way," Bob told Andy. "Don't bring anyone."

Andy turned to Ellen. "Bill Cashill is dead."

As Ellen tells me, "The whole floor fell out."

I did not look at the newspaper accounts until I started this project. The *Star-Ledger* headline that next morning was cold: "Cop found dead with bullet in head." If there were any doubt about the circumstances, the *Newark Evening News* cleared it up, "Cop's death held suicide." Both accounts were understandably superficial. That Dad used his .38-caliber service revolver to take his own life was story enough. To explain the forces that drove him to suicide would take a book.

When I first learned that my father was not dying but dead, I felt an odd, unexpected wave of relief. I would not have to worry about him anymore. Burying the worry as deeply as I had, I could never bury it completely. With every news report of a cop shot or stabbed or beaten, the dread would surge to the surface. Going forward, I was free of that. The burden had been lifted. I would not feel that same sense of love and anxiety again until I had children of my own. I think that police families will understand what I am saying.

Until the end of his days, my uncle Bob would tear up on hearing my father's name. "Only a couple of men stand out in my life," says Aunt Ellen. "One was your Dad." As for me, in our fifteen years together, all the memories he left were good ones. Not many sons can say that of their fathers. Tormented as he was at the end, I imagine Dad now in a finer place, one where all the sadness has lifted, one where all the players get to play football on Saturday and all their fathers get to watch, and, at the end of the day, even poor kids from Newark Central get to go to Georgia Tech.

BELOW GRADE

B y the 1960s, the breakdown in public education, not just in Newark but throughout urban America, was becoming too obvious to ignore. The case of Michelle Obama is instructive. Born in 1964, Michelle spent the first six years of her life in Chicago's Parkway Garden Homes, the nation's first cooperatively owned African American housing development. Parkway Gardens was a big deal at the time. When its cornerstone was laid in 1950, the Chicago mayor and both US senators came to witness. The spacious apartments had all the amenities, and middle-class Black professionals vied to get in. Among its early residents were Michelle's parents, the Robinsons. Her mother, Marian, was a stay-at-home mom, and her father, Fraser, worked for the municipal water department, a front for his real job as a precinct captain in the Daley machine.

In 1962, the bright and shiny new Dulles Elementary School opened just a block away from the Robinson home. After sending Michelle's older brother, Craig, there for two years, the Robinsons had seen enough. From their perspective, the problem wasn't the school building. It was the school's students, many of whom came from nearby housing projects. When Michelle was ready to start school, the Robinsons took a risky step. They used the address of Marian's sister in Chicago's middle-class South Shore neighborhood to enroll both Craig and Michelle at Bryn Mawr Elementary, a fifteen-minute drive from Parkway Gardens.

Born to immigrant parents the same year as Michelle, 1964, Carlo Rotella grew up in South Shore. In 2019, the University of Chicago Press published Rotella's unusually bold book about that experience, *The World Is Always Coming to an End*. Now an English professor at Boston College, Rotella understood why the Robinsons were drawn to the neighborhood, given its history "as one of the most physically attractive parts of the South Side, blessed with good housing stock, lovely parks and beaches, convenient public transportation, and a long-established reputation for respectability."[87]

Although their motives were understandable, the Robinsons had committed a class C misdemeanor. If found out, they would have had to reimburse the school district for the cost of tuition. Nor did they get what they bargained for. The heavily Jewish neighborhood was deep in transition. Although South Shore had been the center of Jewish life on Chicago's South Side in the 1950s, by the late 1960s most of the Jews had fled for the same reason the Robinsons were about to flee Parkway Gardens—schools and crime.

"Crime did rise sharply in South Shore during its era of racial turnover," writes Rotella. "Crime had previously been low in South Shore, so it came as a shock when the neighborhood's rate of FBI-designated index crimes—murder, assault, rape, robbery, burglary, larceny, car theft (arson was added later)—soared from well under the citywide average to double and almost triple that average, among the city's highest."[88] As Rotella notes, the Blacks of South Shore blamed the crime spike on what they called "the element," the refugees from the city's public housing projects.

In researching his book and film, *Michelle Obama 2024*, filmmaker Joel Gilbert caught up with Sybil Kayne, the Jewish woman who in 1965 sold Michelle's aunt her South Shore home. "When I asked Mrs. Kayne why she moved," writes Gilbert, "she told me it was because of increasing crime and violence, the most dramatic symptom of which was an assault on her son. Another neighbor told me his family decided to move after their home was broken into and ransacked."[89]

"Various neighbors moved away for all kinds of reasons when I lived in South Shore," writes Rotella of his neighbors, Black and White, "but the way the story of their departure got told often took the form of 'enough is enough' after a gun-point robbery, home invasion, or similar last-straw outrage."[90] Among those who had had enough of South Shore was Donda West. In her book, *Raising Kanye: Life Lessons from the Mother of a Hip-Hop Superstar*, West talks about the moment she realized South Shore had become untenable.

On one memorable occasion during Kanye's preteen years, some older kids demanded that he hand over his bike. When Kanye refused and tried to ride away, one of the kids slashed his bike tire with a knife. "I was through when Kanye told me about it," writes West. "If it wasn't safe for him to ride his bike in the park that backed right up to our backyard, then it was time to move. I began looking for someplace else to live. Call it black flight or whatever, I was ready to go."[91]

By the time Michelle started at Bryn Mawr, the school was largely Black and more than a little chaotic. "When I was in first grade," Michelle writes in her bestselling memoir, *Becoming*, "a boy in my class punched me in the face one day, his fist coming like a comet, full force and out of nowhere." That punch was a sign of things to come. "My second-grade classroom turned out to be a mayhem of unruly kids and flying erasers," adds Michelle.[92] Until Marian Robinson intervened and got her daughter transferred to the school's gifted program, mayhem was the order of the day.

After Michelle's first-grade year, the Robinsons moved into an apartment above Marian's sister. The Parkway Gardens neighborhood had grown too violent. South Shore was not far behind. "In [our] household, there was fear, fear of other people. Just walking around the block to school," Michelle admitted at one forum. "Just walking around the block, you could get your butt kicked if you talked like a white girl."[93]

Not wanting their children to attend the nearly all-Black South Shore High School just a block or two from their home, the Robinsons paid to send Craig to a predominantly White Catholic high school. To afford the tuition, Marian took a job downtown. The Robinsons were not even Catholic. As for Michelle, she attended a selective magnet school more than an hour away by bus.

Responsible parents of all races, the Robinsons included, could see what was happening to America's public schools, and they acted in their children's best interest. Unfortunately for America, Michelle has chosen to insult White parents who made the same decisions her parents made. And White children, unlike Michelle, remained a target no matter how they talked.

In Newark, Ben was one of these White kids. At the beginning of his second-grade year, Ben started at a new public school that was about 50 percent Black. Says Ben, "That's when the violence started." It was not uncommon, he tells me, for Black kids to take his milk money. He was ashamed to tell his mother, but having to tell someone, he confided in an uncle who told him in no uncertain terms never to let those "N-words" take his money. The uncle also taught him how to fight. "Over the next couple of years," says Ben, "violence became a natural part of life." Out of desperation, Ben's mother transferred him to a well-integrated Catholic school although she, like Michelle's mother, was not Catholic. "Attending Catholic school was the best thing that could have happened for me," says Ben. "It was rough at first, like going from 'See Dick run, run, run, run,' to reading Greek philosophy."

Unfortunately, few people in authority wanted to see what the parents saw happening in America's cities. In his generally insightful book, Newark civil rights activist Robert Curvin cannot quite bring himself to tackle the most critical issue head-on. After decrying the overcrowding of the classrooms, the inexperience of the teachers, and the shortage of textbooks, Curvin mentions, almost as an afterthought, "The influx of black students, many of them from families recently arrived from the South, challenged the cultural and professional aptitude of the teaching corps."

Aptitude of the teaching corps? Black social critic Shelby Steele answers those like Curvin who reflexively excuse the poor performance of Black students. "Isn't the larger problem," writes Steele, "the fact that they come from a subculture—generated in good measure by post-sixties welfare policies—in which nothing serious or difficult is asked of anyone?"[94]

The better teachers struggled to make their classes work despite these students. Pat, a 1964 Barringer grad, went back to the classroom as a teacher after college. "That's when I saw the change," he tells me. It was more change than he was prepared to deal with. He gave up teaching for only slightly more dangerous work as a Newark cop.

Hannah Litzky stuck it out longer. Up until the 1960s, she was thrilled to teach at Weequahic, calling her relationship with the school and its students "a love affair." Her husband was principal at Newark's South Side High School. "He felt a very strong commitment, as I did always, to Newark," she told author William Helmreich. "We wanted integration to work. But when we began to be threatened by the violence and the crime, we just couldn't stay any longer."[95] The violence against teachers was occasionally orchestrated. The *New York Times* reported in a shocking front page story from February 1971, "About 15 striking men and women teachers were beaten to the ground with clubs and fists in a swift attack today by a band of 25 Negro men."[96]

The Litzkys, like other Jews, did not want to run. They did not feel good about it. But run they did. Of the 415 graduates pictured in Weequahic High's 1970 yearbook, only 15 were White—just 3 percent—and only a few of those Jewish. In the activity photos featuring underclassmen I saw no Whites at all. Recall that in 1958 there were only a "handful" of Blacks in Sherry Ortner's graduating class. In *Inside Newark*, Robert Curvin identifies only the neighborhoods that Jews dominated—without making any reference to their Jewishness—as having been "block-busted." As is the norm among such critics, he provides no local documentation of the same.[97]

By contrast, Barringer's 1970 class was 49 percent White. In its own way, Barringer still worked, in part because parents and students expected less of their schools than did the Jews of Weequahic. "Surprisingly I found Barringer to have real teachers who cared," says Lester, who attended in the 1960s. "My first day at Barringer I remember one teacher who said if you don't want to learn, he had no problem if you sat in the back and slept as long as you didn't disrupt the class. What a concept!"

"There was not much of a problem between the races from fall 1961 to June '64," my school friend Frank tells me. As late as 1964, he believes Blacks made up about 12 percent of the Barringer population. My friend Tony, who graduated in 1964, remembers it being "ninety percent Italian." It was never quite that, but it must have seemed that way.

The numbers changed with the opening of the new school building in the fall of 1964 and the busing in of a large contingent of students from the nearly all-Black South Side High. "Trouble was almost immediate," says Frank. "Scuffles in hallways, on the stairs and jockeying for seating in class led to frequent fights after school and finally the Cafeteria Riot where the room interrupted into a free-for-all." Things settled down enough for a Black friend to write in Frank's 1965 yearbook.

"Remember the Riots, Ha Ha," but the riots to come would be no laughing matter.

"I admired Italians," a Newark refugee tells me. "They kept their culture. They didn't take shit," which may explain why they held on to their schools and neighborhoods longer than did Jews. Writes Rotella of his heavily Jewish neighborhood, "South Shore was too middle class, educated, and liberal to go in for the rough stuff."[98]

"Not to be ignored is the collective psychology of Jews in America," writes Helmreich in his history of Jewish Newark. "When faced with the choice of leaving or staying and fighting, they leave."[99] Philip Roth would not have bought that explanation. In his novels, he explored the reasons why Weequahic ceased to be a haven for Newark's Jews, chief among them was their dependence on public schools that could no longer honor their culture's uniquely high standards.

In his 1998 novel *I Married a Communist*, Roth dramatizes the plight of the well-intentioned Jewish teacher through the eyes of Murray Ringold, the brother of the "Communist" in the title. After being sidelined during the McCarthy era, Murray goes back to teaching at Weequahic in the 1960s, "where already, by then, teaching was no picnic." He is then asked to take over the English Department at South Side. "It was even worse," Murray tells the book's narrator, Nathan Zuckerman. "Nobody could teach these black kids, and so they asked me to. I spent the last ten years there, until I retired. Couldn't teach anybody anything. Barely able to hold down the mayhem, let alone teach."[100] Today, not even a fictional teacher would dare speak as candidly as Murray Ringold.

VICTIMHOOD

I n 1924, Congress passed and President Calvin Coolidge signed into law the Johnson-Reed Act. Going forward, annual immigration would be limited to 2 percent of the total number of people of each nationality as recorded on the 1890 census. The act all but dammed the flow of southern and eastern European immigrants into the United States.

The law took no one by surprise. Congress had begun to pare back immigration in 1917 by requiring literacy tests and increasing the cost of admission for would-be immigrants. If these men were conspiring to preserve White male hegemony, they made a botch of it. In June 1919, most of these same men passed the Nineteenth Amendment granting women the right to vote. History is more nuanced than some would like to admit.

Although Johnson-Reed checked Italian and Jewish immigration, it had no effect on the migration of Southern Blacks. A 1931 *New York Times* article, "Negro Population Doubled in Newark," noted the consequences of these opposing trends. While the Black population in Newark increased 129 percent between 1920 and 1930, the "white population" increased just 1.4 percent.[101] By 1931, as evident in the *Times* article, the media made no distinction among European ethnic groups. All were now officially "white."

This blurring of distinctions was, at its core, a sign of progress. It affirmed the Protestant establishment's embrace of a melting pot America. In a city like Newark, however, it had the potential of reducing the power dynamics among ethnic groups to a stark black and white.

The four viable political ethnic blocs in post-war Newark—Italian, Irish, Jewish, and Black—still had distinct subcultures. By the 1960s, each of the groups, save for African Americans, had elected at least one of their own as mayor. Since no group could claim a majority of the voters, power came from reaching across ethnic lines and forming coalitions. The winning candidates inevitably did just that, including Hugh Addonizio, who was elected mayor in 1962.

Each of the four ethnic groups had solid historic claims of victimization, but until the 1960s victimhood had not been part of the power equation. The horrors visited on the world's Jews during World War II, for instance, did not make Jews any more electable in post-war Newark. There were many variables at play in achieving political and economic power, but group suffering was not among them. It was understood that all ethnic groups in America, from the seventeenth-century Dutch onward, had suffered some abuse along the way.

Only for Blacks, however, was the abuse unfolding in real time. Beginning in the late 1950s, the major television networks broadcast images of that abuse on a near nightly basis. The enforcers of Jim Crow may have been as alien to us in

Newark as the despots that sent our ancestors packing, but the media put these enforcers on team "White" just as they did us.

Robert Curvin had seen enough to know the difference between North and South. Curvin's background was pure Horatio Alger. Born in 1934 to a laborer father and a seamstress mother, Curvin grew up with his seven siblings in a largely Italian neighborhood in Belleville, a few blocks from the Newark border. The same age as Amiri Baraka and Philip Roth, Curvin might have met them at Rutgers Newark had he gone straight out of high school as they did. Instead, he enlisted in the US Army and served as a paratrooper with the 101st Airborne Division. After five-plus years of service, he left the Army as a first lieutenant with all the benefits of the GI Bill. He graduated in 1960 from Rutgers, New Jersey's state university.

Curvin was not exactly a pioneer. In 1892, Rutgers graduated its first Black student. A quarter century later, Paul Robeson graduated from Rutgers as valedictorian. The famed Black actor and athlete (and, alas, Stalinist) came to Rutgers well prepared, having attended integrated New Jersey public schools in the years preceding his arrival on campus. Although both were state universities, Rutgers was light-years ahead of, say, the University of Alabama. Three years after Curvin graduated from Rutgers, Alabama Governor George Wallace was grandstanding at the very doors of his state university, denying Black students entrance.

From the mid-1960s onward, however, Black activists took a perverse pleasure in insisting, as famed author James Baldwin did in 1963, "For the negro, there is no difference between the North and South. It's just a difference in the way they castrate you."[102] In fact, many activists and more and more media people consciously attempted to suppress all signs of progress or racial reconciliation.

There was much to suppress. By the 1950s, major institutions, with the military and academia in the lead, were actively advancing the careers of ambitious Blacks like Curvin and Baraka. Writing from a Black nationalist perspective some thirty years after the fact, Baraka recounts, with a smirk, the life choices of his fellow Howard University students. "At least five of us became generals, and many more at lower levels," he writes. "An admiral or two. Reagan's top Negro. Agnew's top Negro. Negroes at all levels of state bureaucracy and madness."[103]

Curvin returned to Newark after leaving the Army. Save for four years at Princeton pursuing his PhD, he lived in Newark until his death in 2015. A civil rights activist and scholar, Curvin published *Inside Newark* a year before he died. The book is an indispensable guide to what the subtitle describes as Newark's "Search for Transformation," a search that Curvin helped lead.

As Curvin notes, Newark's Black population continued to grow after 1930. By 1950, it had reached 17 percent of the city's total. By 1960, it reached 34 percent. That 34 percent, however, did not translate into 34 percent of political power or college degrees or good jobs. Curvin writes, for instance, of Newark's SMSA in 1950, "Approximately one-third the percentage of black males as compared to white males worked in finance, insurance, and real estate."[104]

This may be true, but there were clearly factors at play that Curvin and virtually all other analysts refused to see. The strangling of European immigration in the 1920s meant that, by 1950, there were few unschooled ethnic newcomers moving into the older, less desirable neighborhoods. The European immigrants still in Newark were, on average, older, more literate, more settled, and better assimilated than Black migrants still flowing into the city from the South.

Curvin also complains of only "token progress" for Blacks in city government in the first two decades after World War II,[105] but for the Irish there was no progress at all. Despite JFK's election in 1960, the mayoral election of 1962 meant an end to the Irish bloc as a political force in Newark. Jews, who had generally eschewed electoral politics in any case, were losing political power by the day as their landsmen left for the suburbs, and Italians only *seemed* to be in the ascendancy. Blacks, who had allied with Italians into the 1960s, already outnumbered them and, as their young came of age, would soon be able to out-vote them.

From the 1960s to this very day, Blacks would employ a creative new tool in their quest for power, victimhood. In his role as first chairman of the Newark-Essex Congress of Racial Equality (CORE), Curvin took a prominent part in mobilizing that moral force for targeted ends. In 1963, CORE joined a coalition that, writes Curvin, "called for at least 50 percent minority representation on all municipal construction jobs to make up for the imbalance that had existed for many decades."[106]

In this action, waged over the construction of the new Barringer High School, the unions eventually compromised on a less defined quota, but the strategy set a precedent. Later that same year, Curvin and his CORE colleagues took the fight to AT&T, demanding more jobs for Blacks or "the organization would take direct action." That action included occupying the phone booths at Newark Airport and holding signs explaining why. Under media pressure, AT&T soon buckled.[107]

In 1963, hiring people who themselves never suffered "to make up for" a historical imbalance seemed to many a radical idea. In time, governments, local and national, grew comfortable with the concept. The Civil Rights Act of 1964 was passed to prevent discrimination on the basis of race, color, religion, sex, or national origin, but power politics on the streets of Newark rendered the law obsolete almost as soon as it was enacted.

Despite their often woeful histories, the Irish, Italians, Jews, and others were never offered the perks of victimhood. This was as it should have been. Rewarding members of one group meant punishing members of another, a strategy sure to create friction wherever applied. To meet the demands of Black activists, however, feckless civic leaders were prepared to ignore the Civil Rights Act and sacrifice the aspirations of young working-class ethnics—cops, firemen, school teachers, construction workers—to "make up for" a history they had no part in shaping. For all his savvy, Curvin seemed indifferent to those who would pay the price for Blacks to achieve "equity." Spoiler alert: it wasn't the AT&T brass or their children.

The media, now drawing new recruits from liberal journalism schools, chose not to see urban power struggles in their multicultural complexity. They preferred simple melodramas in black and white, with White ethnics assigned the role of the oppressor, a role that had to shock those old enough to remember clambering, broke and bewildered, from the ships that dropped them off on America's shores.

PAYBACK TIME

"**E**xtensive scholarship argues that urban violence has its roots in poverty," Robert Curvin, among others, has argued.[108] Alexis de Tocqueville would disagree. "It is not always by going from bad to worse that a society falls into a revolution," de Tocqueville wrote of his native France a century to the year before the Montgomery Bus Boycott. "It happens most often that a people, which has supported without complaint, as if they were not felt, the most oppressive laws, violently throws them off as soon as their weight is lightened."[109]

In the 1960s, the spirit of revolution filtered down to the streets of Newark and other American cities. Despite huge progress on the civil rights front—or perhaps because of it—young Blacks seemed edgier and angrier than I remembered. It is hard to show progress on television, but the imagery of billy clubs and fire hoses needed little in the way of explanation. Now living in New York City, Amiri Baraka had caught the spirit. He writes of that time and place, "In my fury, which had no scientific framework, I could only thrash out at any white person."[110]

I got the sense that it was payback time. In my eighth-grade year, 1961, St. Rose had to stagger its start and end times to avoid attacks on our students, mostly White, by those from Roseville Avenue School, mostly Black. We never had to do that before. I could particularly feel the vibe on the heavily Black basketball courts where I misspent my adolescence. Having peaked early at six-foot and nearly two hundred pounds, I had no greater asset than heft. Where heft in motion once netted comments such as, "Man, you hellfire under the boards," these soon turned to veiled threats like, "This ain't Mississippi, motherfucker."

John D. traced his first incident back to 1961 as well. The third of eleven children of Quebecois immigrants, John was a classic free-range child. One day, while walking to a Salvation Army store to buy shoes, he spotted a hammer-wielding Black man running toward him yelling something about "a little White motherfucker." John, being the only little White person in the vicinity, presumed that the motherfucker in question had to be himself. He took off running, jumping over car hoods and dodging traffic to elude the guy. He was eleven at the time.

A gifted storyteller, John has put many of his stories in writing. His father, like mine, bought a home in 1954, a half of a duplex about a mile south of where we lived. The main drag in his neighborhood was South Orange Avenue, and for the first seven or so years the family lived there John thought it "the promised land." He can still list all the stores up and down the street that he and his brothers freely explored. "It was absolutely beautiful at that time," he tells me.

Bill and Sandy Christie thought so too. They lived on South Orange Avenue just three short blocks west of John.

Their marriage was classic Newark. Bill was Irish on his father's side, German on his mother's. Sandy was Sicilian on both. "My parents were Newarkers. They didn't want to go," their son Chris writes about Bill and Sandy. But, as Chris acknowledges, "Newark was really on the edge. Crime was rising. Racial tension was growing." The Christies stuck it out until 1966 when they borrowed money from their parents and bought a home in Livingston, eighteen miles to the west. "You're taking me to the sticks," Sandy griped to her husband, but she went anyhow with four-year-old Chris in tow. Chris would later become the governor of New Jersey.[111]

In an oddly comic story that John D. has titled, "You Got Any Caramels," John recounts an incident that makes the Christies' departure fully understandable. It was Halloween 1962. John was a small twelve. He rushed home from school to find his mother applying "pink medicine" to three of his brothers. They all had ringworm. He was on his own to trick-or-treat with the added obligation of securing extra booty for his ailing brothers. John details his many adventures that night including a trip to the basement of a funeral home where "Lurch," guiding him past the dead bodies, gives him a six-pack of Coca-Cola, a major coup for a trick-or-treater.

"There was only one thing I did not do on this day," John admits. "I did not have my radar on." He paid the price. Five Black teens, females, spotted him as he headed home and crossed the street toward him. Out of nowhere, without a word said, the ringleader punched him in the head. "BANG! I went to the ground," writes John. "Next, they all come like a raging storm, the Bristol Stomp—the Watusi and the Mash

Potato on my curled-up body pleading for mercy. It lasted and lasted till I manage to crawl away. I got home bloodied and battered." That was the last time John went trick-or-treating in Newark.

Females could be as rough as males. Maggie, who left Roseville at eleven when the freeway came through, tells me she was attacked by gangs of older Black girls "all the time." When I ask her what "all the time" meant, she answers, "probably six times." For an eleven-year-old, six safely qualifies as "all the time." What triggered the attacks, she believes, was her blonde hair. Black girls seemed to take special pleasure in pulling it. Although there is something truly sad about attacks like these, preteen victims lack the wherewithal to excuse them. Parents of little girls are even less forgiving, which is why Maggie, like many kids in the neighborhood, chose not to tell her parents. She feared they would only restrict her freedom of movement.

Renee tells the story of walking to Branch Brook Park in the company of a male friend as small as she was. They were on their way to the ice skating rink when a Black girl wearing a fedora approached with a group of her friends. The girl put her arm around Renee's shoulder and asked, "Where are you going?" There was never a right answer to these setup questions.

Says Renee, "She socked me." Renee called the police when she got to the rink. Apparently, she and her friend were not the only White kids who had been attacked that day, but there was little the Newark PD could do for them. The city's problems were already well beyond its power.

ASSISTED SUICIDE

Although Whites were often the victims, young Blacks turned much of their rage against one another. Michelle Obama talks about her taunting by Black girls at some length in *Becoming*. In one instance the harassment led to fist-icuffs. "When she made that remark," writes Michelle of her tormentor, "I lunged for her, summoning everything my dad had taught me about how to throw a punch."[112] The daughter of a Black woman who lived in Michelle's neighborhood had a comparable experience. Said the mother, explaining to Carlo Rotella why she was about to flee South Shore, "And I have to keep runnin' up to the school to make sure my daughter is safe. She can't concentrate on school because she was gettin' beat up every other day."[113]

"What part did having attitudes of superiority or superior goals play?" George Langston Cook of Columbus Homes asks of his friends and siblings who fell prey to the prevailing unease. "Or was the primary cause the frustration of not being able to achieve those lofty ambitions? Were these the cause for such a level of human failure?"

Born in 1952, Cook began to feel the mood change in the Columbus Homes around 1960. Under pressure from activist groups, the Newark Housing Authority (NHA) cut back on home inspections. As a result, says Cook with regret, "Fewer evictions resulted."[114] By the early 1960s, drug use was epidemic in the project. So, consequently, was crime. "Some went so far as to pull stick-ups at a nearby commuter train station or rob bus drivers," writes Cook of the druggies. "For the first time it was not safe to be alone in Columbus' halls, as muggings became common place."

Crime was not limited to the Columbus Homes. "Older women shopping on the avenue or on Broadway fell victim to drug related crime as heroin addicts snatched pocketbooks," notes Cook. "An atmosphere of fear hung over the neighborhood because of these assaults."[115] The fear of crime drove many of the remaining Italians out of the projects as well as the surrounding neighborhood. Private landlords rented to whomever they could and did not invest in upkeep. Arson became routine, and many of those burned out of their homes fled the neighborhood, never to return. Others turned to the Newark Housing Authority for sanctuary, and, rues Cook, "Columbus became more of a haven for welfare-dependent families."

Crime was taking its toll on the physical property of the project as well. Light bulbs were snatched from the hallways. Windows were broken. Elevators were vandalized. Trash receptacles were swiped. As a result, maintenance staff was spread thin, as were maintenance dollars. "Littering in the neighborhood increased," writes Cook. "Paper wrappers, cans, and trash generated outside apartments, ended up on the ground. Broken glass became common on the sidewalks and playgrounds. Cigarette butts were found everywhere."[116]

These signs of communal decay were equally visible in Chicago's South Shore a few years later. Michelle Obama's brother, Craig, spoke openly of the deterioration of their neighborhood. "You slowly saw these parks where we used to play in the sandbox," said Craig at a public forum with his sister, "and then each year, you'd find more and more bottles, and more and more glass broken, and it was like people didn't care about the parks. They didn't care about where we went to play."[117]

What is refreshing about Cook's heartfelt book, *The War Zone*, is that he writes about what he knows and rarely generalizes beyond what the physical evidence supports. In the section of the book called "War Stories," Cook profiles the lives of more than sixty acquaintances from Columbus Homes, almost all of whom yielded to the increasing self-destructive neighborhood culture. Some brief excerpts:

ଔ

Michael's life was taken by his mother's paramour, shot down while he was in a fit of anger, threatening death himself, and wreaking havoc in their home.

ଔ

There was nothing Eddie and his sisters seemed afraid to try…. One by one they died.

ଔ

They tell me Tommy died when he fell from the subway platform in front of a moving subway car in New York City.

❧

Keith eventually died by the time he was 36, supposedly due to AIDS.

❧

Billy died in a pool of his own blood with a hypodermic needle lodged in his arm.

❧

What we do know is that Andre died from the injury and Walter returned to jail.

❧

Bruce was shot dead by three teenage punks outside of a store near Springfield Avenue following an argument that took place inside.

❧

Willie fell hard into the drug life, right around the time I went into the service.

❧

David, age eleven, honor roll student, dead.

Cook writes of numerous others who were found dead of overdoses, shot dead on the streets, or locked away in prison. Although he had no answers, Amiri Baraka, nearly twenty years older than Cook, recognized the difference between their respective childhoods. "But when you fought you did not expect anybody to have a knife, let alone a piece," Baraka writes. "When today the pulling of shanks is normal, and guns, just about."[118] For all the words he has spoken or written, Baraka never explains what made Black life so much more dangerous in so short a time.

Among the "wounded" in the Columbus Homes were several of Cook's brothers. In years gone by, he might have been justified in writing off their failures to White oppression, but as George and brother Jimmy both knew, that excuse no longer applied. An above average student, "Jimmy could accomplish anything he wanted to," writes Cook. It was his "arrogance," he believes, that led Jimmy to drugs. Drug use caused Jimmy to drop out of college and lose a job at the post office that his father helped secure. "His life," writes Cook, "became one of unfulfilled potential."

The potential was real. After fifteen years of a squandered life, Jimmy looked within and did not like what he saw. He went back to college, completed a degree in computer science, and, at the time of the book's publication, was managing computer systems on Wall Street. A few other Columbus Home vets also pulled themselves out of the death spiral. Bernard, more typically perhaps, "reattached himself to his faith, his belief in God, and put up a battle with addiction to make us proud."

What saved George was the US Navy. After his father left home when he was a teen, Cook started drinking, even during class. He enlisted in the Navy during the Vietnam years, "just hoping to get away from home." After the Navy, he went back to college and graduated from Arizona State. Cook returned to Newark because his mother was dying and remained there, working a variety of useful jobs in social services. Perhaps more importantly, he saw enough of Newark to write an unusually valuable book about a dying city.

As an adolescent in the early 1960s, I had yet to sense in full the city's decline, but there was no mistaking the increase in tensions between Blacks and Whites. In the 1962–63 season, my friends and I entered a team—the grandly named "Utopian A.C."—in the Sussex Avenue School sixteen-and-under league. Most of us were fifteen, and all of us, save our friend Tyrone, were White. Tyrone was a wonder. Uniquely indifferent to race, he thought it no big deal to be the only Black guy on the only White team in a racially contentious league.

What made Tyrone's life more difficult was that we were winning. In fact, we won the league. More than a few times, though, we found ourselves backing out of the gym after a game to avoid attack, running up Sussex Avenue, and breathing easy only once we passed the Italian tough guys hanging out on the corner of Fourth Street. The fact that they kept a weight bench right on the sidewalk served as a deterrent. God may have made the world round, but thankfully he allowed for streets to have corners.

Years later, I appeared on Stephen A. Smith's ESPN show, *Quite Frankly*, to discuss *Sucker Punch*, my book on childhood hero Muhammad Ali. Another guest asked me if I ever participated in a civil rights march. "Yeah, every day," I answered. "Every day that I walked to the playground and back without getting my ass kicked, that was my civil rights march."

WILLFUL BLINDNESS

n 1963, an older couple who lived a few houses down from us, the Henneberrys, moved out. Their single-family home, like ours, was in the freeway's path, and no family would buy it. The three Black single moms who rented it came with sixteen kids in tow. On a warm spring night, these kids generated more noise than a swarm of cicadas. Soon after, the Farleys moved out from across the street, and a comparable collective moved in. Now, we had the cicadas in stereo.

Among the sixteen kids were two boys my age, Pete and Lance. I got to know them a little. We played some touch football in the street and ran into each other at the Sussex Avenue gym. They smelled like urine—not sure why—but otherwise were okay. They had a friend who wasn't. The first time I encountered the friend, he challenged me to a fight right in front of my own house. I couldn't overlook the thick metal rings on his fingers, at least three on each hand. "Take the rings off," I said, "and let's go." He refused my request, and so nothing happened. Just as well, but Myrtle Avenue suddenly wasn't what it used to be.

America wasn't either. In November 1963, of course, John F. Kennedy was assassinated. It was not until decades later that it dawned on me that my two heroes died in the same calendar year, each from the same cause, a bullet to the brain. JFK was born a year before my father and lived ten months after my father died. Ten months is a long time in the life of a fifteen-year-old.

Switching allegiance to Kennedy's successor, Lyndon Johnson, did not come easily. On style, which mattered more than it should have, LBJ was not in JFK's league. Nor was he Irish or Catholic. I would, however, find one Mick in Johnson's administration with style and moxie to spare. As assistant secretary of labor, Daniel Patrick Moynihan issued a report in 1965 that shook the nation's capital more viscerally than any document since the "Pumpkin Papers." Upon reading *The Negro Family: The Case for National Action*[119] in a sociology class years later, I understood why the report so upset official Washington. Moynihan had told the truth about what we were seeing in the streets and playgrounds. Family breakdown was a reality of which most good deed-doing bureaucrats remained oblivious.

Despite the "full recognition of their civil rights," argues Moynihan, Blacks were increasingly discontent. They were expecting that equal opportunities would "produce roughly equal results, as compared with other groups," but adds Moynihan, "This is not going to happen." Nor did he think it ever would happen "unless a new and special effort is made." In explaining the primary cause of the already widening achievement gap between Blacks and Whites, Moynihan went where few elected officials have ever dared to go:

> The fundamental problem, in which this is most
> clearly the case, is that of family structure. The

evidence—not final, but powerfully persuasive—
is that the Negro family in the urban ghettos is
crumbling. A middle class group has managed to
save itself, but for vast numbers of the unskilled,
poorly educated city working class the fabric
of conventional social relationships has all but
disintegrated.

Columbus Homes served as an involuntary lab for
Moynihan's theories. By the 1960s, few families in that project had a married father in the home. Even author George
Cook's father abandoned the family. "Negro children without
fathers flounder—and fail," writes Moynihan only a shade too
broadly. "White children without fathers at least perceive all
about them the pattern of men working." On my block, just
a mile away, the pattern of men working was unmistakable.
The 1950 census recorded just two female-headed households
out of eighty-three on Myrtle Avenue. Of the eighty-one male
heads, seventy-nine had a job. Fatherlessness was rare to the
point of being newsworthy—in my case, literally.

In 1950, Black neighborhoods were not quite as solid,
but they were close. Before the 1960s, among Black families,
Aid to Families with Dependent Children (AFDC) cases and
employment numbers rose and fell in near perfect harmony:
the lower the unemployment rate, the fewer the AFDC cases.
In 1960, "for the first time" as Moynihan points out, unemployment numbers declined, but the number of new AFDC
cases rose. This seemingly freakish pattern repeated itself in
1963 and again in 1964. More jobs no longer meant fewer
people dependent on government assistance. This unwelcome

development put pressure on government resources, but that was a minor problem compared to the damage done to family and community stability.

"The principal challenge of the next phase of the Negro revolution is to make certain that equality of results will now follow," writes Moynihan at his most prescient. "If we do not, there will be no social peace in the United States for generations." The report received solid support when circulated within the Johnson administration, but when released publicly in July 1965, Johnson wilted under fire from civil rights activists of the type Shelby Steele describes as "opportunists living off the moral authority of black suffering."[120] Johnson cancelled a conference he had scheduled around the idea of family and scolded his staffers for getting him "in this controversy over Moynihan." Writes Daniel Geary in his book on the Moynihan report, "After November [1965] it was effectively dead as a source for White House policy."[121]

Moynihan's sin was to see what others refused to. When earlier waves of Black migrants came to Newark from the South, they understood, just as European immigrants understood, that to survive one had to *make* a living. Baraka and Cissy Houston attest to just how responsible and hardworking their parents were even in an environment that was often unwelcoming.

The waves of Southern migrants that came to Newark starting in the mid-1950s were met by social workers eager to show how a living could be had without being made. The benefits they offered came at a cost. The 1967 report issued by the Select Commission for the Study of Civil Disorder in New

Jersey—the *Hughes Report* for short—observes of AFDC, "If the father stays home, the family is not eligible, even though the father may be unemployed or earn an amount far below the needs of the family." That is accurate enough. Post-Moynihan, the report authors knew better than to address the fallout from welfare dependency head on. Instead, they attribute such talk to unnamed "critics of the system."[122] By 1967, almost no one in Washington was willing to say the obvious out loud.

In getting to know my new neighbors, Lance and Pete, I wondered even then how they could ever hope to escape the chaos that engulfed them. Scarier still, these two were no longer outliers. In places like Columbus Homes, they had become the norm. In Newark, kids like Lance and Pete would be competing against young White ethnics—Irish, Jewish, Italian—whose family stability rates were even higher than the national average for Whites, more than 90 percent in each case.

Once official Washington chose to ignore Moynihan's findings, federal and state authorities could continue in good conscience to provide more incentives for young men to leave home. AFDC was the door opener. In 1964, the feds sweetened the pot for forsaken moms with food stamps and in 1965 with Medicaid. Shortly afterwards, public housing switched from fixed rents to rents based on family income, a change that made a married father even more of a pariah.

Robert Curvin's book *Inside Newark* testifies to Moynihan's irrelevance in civil rights circles. Curvin does not mention Moynihan. Nor does he use the phrases "fatherless," "wedlock," "illegitimate," or "family breakdown." Despite his savvy, Curvin prefers to talk about jobs, here lapsing into tired clichés. "As in many cities throughout America," he writes, "Newark's racial and ethnic divisions were more than symbolic; they were rooted in an active and intense competition for scarce jobs and perquisites in a declining urban economy."[123]

If there was any city whose evolution paralleled Newark's in the 1960s, it was Gary, Indiana. In fact, Gary elected its first Black mayor in 1967, three years before Newark did. Jesse Lee Peterson, a friend and conservative activist, spent much of his adolescence in Gary. What he witnessed there subverts the liberal orthodoxy preached by Curvin and others.

Born in rural Alabama in 1949 and raised largely by his grandparents, Peterson started coming to Gary in 1960 to visit the mother who had abandoned him. "If there was one thing obviously missing from the lives of my Indiana peers, it was respect," writes Peterson in his essential book, *The Antidote*. "In Alabama, our elders demanded respect, and we gave it. Knowing its value, we gave respect to one another as well."[124] Each year, Peterson came back to visit; he could sense the change in Gary, and the change was not for the better. "By the mid-1960s," he adds, "the welfare culture had settled in to Gary, and respect was breaking down."

Peterson traces White flight not to some paranoid anxiety about the "other," but to a legitimate fear of bad actors. "There were some scary guys in Gary back then, and their bad behavior forced other kids to adapt," writes Peterson. "I began to wonder how white people must have felt. They saw what I saw, and they had options." In 1967, he moved to Gary full time and attended Thomas A. Edison High School. "I had never lived among black kids that were so violent," he notes. "I had not grown up like that."[125]

Peterson was in Gary the year Richard Hatcher was elected mayor. He had hoped that Hatcher's election would ease the tension he felt in the school hallways. It did not. "It empowered the black kids to act out even more," he observes, "giving them permission to ramp up their attacks on non-blacks."

In watching Gary disintegrate over the years, Peterson has refused to buy the argument that a contracting economy caused Black family and community breakdown. "This, of course, is all backwards," he argues. "The black community in Gary was collapsing during the 1960s while jobs went begging in the steel mills. I know this firsthand. In 1968, as an inexperienced eighteen-year-old, I got a well-paying job at Inland Steel without half trying."[126]

The numbers would seem to prove out Peterson's thesis. During the 1950s, Moynihan points out, the ratio of non-white to White family income in cities increased from 57 to 63 percent. Starting in 1960, the trend reversed, and the gap between Black and White income began to grow. The gap was particularly pronounced, says Moynihan, among the young "caught up in the tangle of pathology that affects their world." Cook documented this pathology at Columbus Homes just as Peterson did in Gary. They saw what we saw in Roseville. The economy wasn't the problem. The problem was young people unwilling or unable to hold a job.

In arguably his finest novel, *American Pastoral*, Philip Roth tells the story of Seymour "the Swede" Levov, a legendary high school athlete out of Weequahic. For years, Levov ran his family glove-manufacturing company, Newark Maid, in the city that lent the company its name. The Swede's father and company founder, Lou Levov, saw problems ahead. As early as 1964, he was urging his son to move the company out of Newark. Choosing to live with "the erosion of the workmanship" among his Black employees, the liberal-minded Swede resists his father's advice. A weeklong sequence of events in 1973 finally breaks the Swede's resistance. A Black employee is shot right in front of the business. A woman is killed nearby. And Swede himself is the victim of a carjacking. "That week did it," says Swede. "That was enough."[127]

Despite massive evidence to the contrary, the media prefer to blame fleeing Whites for the economic decline of cities like Newark and Gary. A headline of a 2017 article in the *Guardian*, a prominent British newspaper, nicely captures progressive confusion on the subject: "White flight followed factory jobs out of Gary, Indiana. Black people didn't have a choice."[128] In fact, White flight *preceded* the layoffs by U.S. Steel, which began in 1971. As late as 1970, the company employed more than thirty thousand people. Whites left because they lived with what Peterson saw, and they didn't like it. Many Black residents of Gary left for the exact same reason. By 2010, the city had nearly one hundred thousand fewer residents than it did in 1970 when it was a majority-Black city with a Black mayor.

The *Guardian* editors descend into the realm of the unserious with their claim, "Black people didn't have a choice." Of course Black people had a "choice," and many exercised it. The article quotes at least two African Americans who moved away and returned only to take care of aging parents. The *Guardian* gives the money quote to a Puerto Rican woman who reminisces fondly about her White ethnic neighbors before reverting to media-friendly self-praise. "Then in 1981, people started moving out. They started seeing black people coming in, and they said they would bring drugs and crime, so they left. I stayed because I don't judge by color."

That same article, however, quotes a Black Gary resident who all but boasts that Gary had become "the murder capital of the US" and the "drug capital" as well. He was not making stuff up. A January 1994 *Chicago Tribune* article ran with the headline, "Gary Takes Over as Murder Capital of U.S." That year, Gary's murder rate was three times higher than even Chicago's.[129] In this dubious category, Newark is a perennial in the top ten, a source of pride among more than a few locals.

OVER THE BRIDGE

In the summer of 1954, with a new baby at home, my mother decided to send Bob and me to camp. I was six at the time. Bob was seven. The minimum age for Camp Kiamesha was eight. Mom instructed both of us to tell the YMCA people we were eight and nine respectively. My mother was age-fluid. For her, you were as old as you needed to be. Bob remembered he was nine. I forgot and said I was six until Mom nudged me, and I remembered I was eight. The camp guy pretended not to notice, and off we went for two weeks in the New Jersey wilderness, me the youngest kid in camp by two years except for Bob.

I took well to camp life. At ages eight, nine, and ten, I went to Camp Brady, a Newark Boys Club camp. And at ages eleven, twelve, and thirteen, I went to Camp Mohican, a Boy Scout camp. The summer I was fourteen I stayed home to play baseball. In that time and place, parents didn't run our lives. They rarely even went to our games. In the two leagues in which I played that summer, I was the catcher and our team's closest thing to a coach. We had no real coach. We had no chauffeur.

On that summer's most memorable day, we started with a game in a city league at School Stadium. Only when we got there did we learn the water fountain was on the fritz. Our next game in the Police Athletic League (PAL) followed immediately afterwards. We ran in a herd from School Stadium to the PAL field about a mile and a half away. At each tavern en route we stuck our heads in and begged for water. Each and every bartender turned us away. When we finally got to the PAL field, we dove into the water buckets like a lost brigade of Foreign Legionnaires. On the positive side, we won both games.

After my father's death the following January, my mother wanted Bob and me out of the city. Billy, the program director at Kiamesha, got us jobs washing dishes in the camp kitchen. It was miserable work and a forgettable summer. I had experience enough, however, to get a job as a counselor the following summer at Camp Brady, the Newark Boys Club camp. I talked my best friend, Kenny, into taking a kitchen job at the same camp.

Kenny's kitchen experience at Brady proved even more miserable than my own at Kiamesha. He had to sleep in an unlit, rat-infested cabin with the kitchen crew down by the river away from the main body of camp. Within a week, he ran away from camp, and, because he took off when he did, his life would change forever in nearly miraculous ways.

Brady was a good camp to run away from. At sixteen, I was its youngest counselor. My unit leader, Dave, a totally cool, crew-cutted rapscallion, kept a .22 rifle by his bedside and would occasionally shoot at the feet of counselors caught sneaking out. Gun safety being what it was, a junior counselor actually shot a camper in the middle of the campground.

The shooter claimed it was an accident. The kid survived. No harm. No foul.

The most troubled unit, the Iroquois, was home to the youngest kids. Unfortunately for the kids, the city's fractious ethnic juju had descended on the countryside. At the center of the storm were two Jewish counselors from the suburbs, both Ivy Leaguers and likely gay. After a second unit leader quit, they decided to bunk together with all fourteen of their charges in a tent designed for eight. If their motive was self-defense, it was justified. What riled the Black staff in particular was less the Jewishness of the pair, or even their presumed gayness, but their inability to hide their intelligence.

Back in Newark, life was no saner. Or safer. One day early in the summer, Kenny got jumped on Sussex Avenue. He gave as good as he got, but one of the three Black assailants knocked out a front tooth. Kenny's father, Frank, had his son identify the culprit. Trying to stay on the right side of the law, Frank had the kid apprehended and taken to court. There, to Frank's disgust, the judge bawled out both the perp and Kenny as though they were equal partners in crime. Infuriated by the treatment, Frank arranged for Kenny to spend the rest of the summer in Brick with his relatives.

That Beatles summer of '64, Kenny met the lovely Denise, then just fifteen, his first and only love, and the civilizing force in his life to this day. After camp season ended and before school started, I went down to hang out and help Kenny paint houses. Broke and carless, I had zero social life in the seriously Catholic confines of Roseville, but the girls in Brick seemed plentiful and, to a point, obliging. I met one

I'll call "Sharon" who, bless her hard little heart, said I looked like Marlon Brando. That was prompting enough for me to promise a return visit.

No sooner did Kenny get back to Newark than he got jumped again. His father had had enough. He pulled Kenny out of his Catholic high school and sent him down to Brick to live with relatives. A few weeks later I kept my promise to Sharon. To set things up, I called her from a pay phone—at home a long-distance call required a written proposal—the day before I was to arrive. On Friday, I took the bus down to Brick over my mother's objections and walked to Sharon's house. There, her mom informed me she had gone to the drive-in with a guy named "Jimmy," real name. Jimmy obviously had a car. Marlon Brando wasn't even old enough to drive.

Seething, and with suitcase in hand, I walked to Kenny's aunt's house only to learn that Kenny forgot to tell her I was coming. As coolly as the innkeeper in Bethlehem, she turned me away. With Kenny working at a burger place, I walked to Denise's house, suitcase still in hand. (We had already put a man in space but had not yet thought to put wheels on suitcases.) Denise's mom invited me in and, together, we watched the premiere of the *Addams Family*. I fact-checked the date. It was September 18, 1964.

Later that night, Kenny found me lodging at another aunt's house, but he had to work all day Saturday. To save face at home, I could not return until Sunday. No big deal. I figured I'd hitchhike up to the beach Saturday morning, find a book to read, and kill a few zits with the sun and the salt. Man plans, as they say, and God laughs. As awful as September

18 was, September 19 was worse. The day's saving grace—
and why I include the story at length—was that it showed
me how life was organized in the instant suburbs of White
flight America. Without that day, I would not have written
this book.

Saturday was monsoon from dawn to dusk. Back in
Roseville on a rainy day, I had two movie theaters within two
blocks, a diner right down the street to hang out in, a church
if I really needed solace, and quick access to a bus downtown
or even to New York City. I never valued my neighborhood
more than I did that rainy Saturday.

Here, in Brick, I had no place to go but Sharon's. She
offered some lame explanation as to why she forgot our Friday
engagement, and I had little choice but to believe her. Sharon
lived with her mother, little sister, and stepfather in a small
ranch house. I had never met a "stepfather" in the wild before.
A local guy, he referred to me contemptuously as "Nickie
Newark" and left the strong impression that he and I were
competing for the same girl.

The day's highlight was a trip with Sharon and her mom
to the "shopping center," a glorified strip mall without a movie
theater or even a diner to hang out in. That night, Sharon had
a babysitting gig, and I went with her. We made out a little,
PG-13 style, but at this point in our relationship, such as it
was, I wished I was back watching *The Addams Family* with
Denise's mom. That, at least, I did in good conscience. Next
morning, first thing, I walked up to the bus station and waited
a few hours for the Newark bus to come. It was still raining.

I spent a lot of time on the letter I sent to Sharon after that visit and still remember some of what I wrote, including my reliance on the prefix "un." Unbound by any code, I argued, Sharon failed to honor a commitment on Friday that she had made on Thursday and seemed untroubled by her failure. She was uncentered, I insisted, because hers was a world without a moral center or even a secular one. The phrase shopping *center* was a trick on displaced people who had no place else to go on a rainy Saturday.

Even at the time, I was struck by the pomposity of my own argument. In retrospect I see the hypocrisy of it as well. Sharon's relative "looseness" is what attracted me in the first place. When she proved to be even looser than I thought—a drive-in with a Jimmy?—I felt obliged to deconstruct the social dynamics that made her loose as though I were somehow above the fray. I wasn't.

That much conceded, my analysis holds. The towns that sprang up in the reclaimed pine barrens of the shore provided housing for the dispossessed but little in the way of community. Many of these new residents had left behind their churches, their neighborhoods, and their extended families only to find themselves in a world without a heartbeat. Lacking sidewalks, front porches, or even stoops, subdivisions did not easily evolve into neighborhoods. People retreated inward, and communal values withered.

The displaced females from Roseville with whom I spoke seemed particularly lost. "I hated it," Renee told me. Forced to move in a hurry during the 1967 riots, she ended up in still another town south of the Raritan. She had gone to an all-girls Catholic high school in Newark but now had to attend a public school. "The girls were afraid of me," she said. "They were very unfriendly, especially to Newarkers." Linda ended up south of the Raritan as well. Being unable to drive in a town with dirt roads and one supermarket did not make for a happy life. She had no family anywhere close, and long-distance rates discouraged friends from calling. "I was very miserable," Linda told me. "I was nineteen. I didn't fit in."

Despite the emotional cost of removal, more St. Rose of Lima alumni from the 1960s—the decade most catastrophic for Roseville—ended up living in the shore counties of Ocean and Monmouth than ended up in Essex, Newark's county.[130] Only a handful from that decade remained in Newark. The presence of the dispossessed helped Trump carry both Monmouth and Ocean Counties in 2016 and 2020. In each of those years, Ocean, Brick's county, proved to be the reddest county in the state. On the boardwalk of the county's most popular resort, Seaside Heights, one shop sold nothing but Trump memorabilia. In an otherwise blue state, Trump won Ocean County both times by a nearly two-to-one margin.

If the motivating issue was crime, the Newark refugees who ended up in Brick chose wisely. In 2006, Brick beat out 370 other cities in the annual Morgan Quitno survey to earn the title "America's Safest City." In 2021, a Newark resident was thirteen times more likely to be murdered than a resident of Brick and eight times more likely to have a car stolen. Brick is perennially the state's safest city of size.

In time, as families established roots, the residents of these instant towns built their own churches and developed their own rituals and traditions. Most of my closest friends from Newark settled in these Shore towns and raised their families there. One friend, Tony, taught in Brick for twenty-five years after starting his teaching career in Newark. He watched Brick mature around him. "Brick was amazing," he says of the town in general and the high school in particular.

When I met five of my closest friends for lunch in the course of this project, we convened in a spot convenient for them all, Wall Township, fifty-five miles south of Newark. As much as they dreaded their commutes while still working, these guys thought the move worth the trade-off. That said, they all conceded that none of their children had as rich and free a childhood as they had enjoyed in Roseville... before the fall.

RUMBLES

It was just one of those days when I couldn't miss. We were playing pickup basketball at the St. Rose playground. In that the winner kept the court, my teammates kept feeding me, and we kept extending the lead.

One guy on my team took exception. "Yeah, give the brother the ball," he snarled, drenching the word "brother" in deep fat-fried irony. "He think he bad." I had never seen this guy before. My teammates looked as confused as I felt. The guy kept at it. "Yeah, he think he better than us. Give the brother the ball." I should add that I was the only White guy on the court, the only White guy in the playground for that matter. It was spring 1965. I was seventeen years old, and change was in the air. That change was rumbling through Black communities across the nation, but in Newark those rumbles were moving the needle on the social Richter scale.

In 1965, the city was the Casablanca of racial intrigue. All manner of questionable characters were passing through or hanging around. My old basketball buddy Dennis tells me he stopped by Don Newcombe's bar on Orange Street about that time looking for an autograph only to find Muhammad Ali in the house. He was flanked, says Dennis, by Nation of Islam (NOI) bodyguards, the so-called Fruit of Islam.

The Nation of Islam traces its roots to Newark. It was there in 1913 that Noble Drew Ali founded the Moorish Science Temple of America, a cult that fused Black nationalism with Islam. Twenty years later, after a series of murder plots and disappearances, Elijah Poole, now "Elijah Muhammad," assumed control of the NOI and eventually settled on Chicago as headquarters.

In 1964, Elijah Mohammad and rising NOI star Louis Farrakhan declared open season on the Nation's most brazenly disloyal apostate, Malcolm X. Among other sins, Malcolm had publicly rejected NOI's anti-White extremism. The Nation did not take rejection well. "Only those who wish to be led to hell, or to their doom, will follow Malcolm," Farrakhan wrote in December 1964. "The die is set, and Malcolm shall not escape.... Such a man as Malcolm is worthy of death."

On February 21, 1965, death came knocking. That morning, the Boston-based Farrakhan just happened to be visiting Newark Mosque No. 25. Opened in 1958, the Newark mosque had nurtured in its members a taste for radicalism and violence. That afternoon, a NOI death squad from that very same mosque headed to the Audubon Ballroom in Harlem and there assassinated Malcolm X in full view of his family. A week after Malcolm's murder, Elijah Muhammad boasted at a Chicago rally that Malcolm's "foolish teaching brought him to his own end." Sitting behind Muhammad and affirming his every word was "brother" Muhammad Ali.[131]

Helping stir the cauldron that year was White brother Tom Hayden—yes, that Tom Hayden, co-founder of the radical Students for a Democratic Society (SDS) and future bride of Jane Fonda. It was Hayden who drafted the celebrated "Port Huron Statement," a manifesto that laid out the foundation for what he dared to call the "new left." In a memo written to his colleagues about the statement, Hayden urged misdirection. "We will be 'out' if we are explicitly socialists, or if we espouse any minority political views honestly," he noted. "We can be further 'in' if we are willing to call socialism liberalism."[132]

In 1964, according to Robert Curvin, Hayden and his SDS colleagues were part of a larger national program "to organize a social movement of poor and working-class people to create fundamental changes in American society." Roseville apparently wasn't working class enough. Hayden never came near us. Eleven of Hayden's SDS group of twelve were White. They were not interested in working with people who looked like them. No romance in that.

The mentor for many of Hayden's people was Chicago's Saul Alinsky, a Marxist savant who would later serve as inspiration for both Hillary Clinton and Barack Obama. Alinsky, writes Amity Shlaes in her book *Great Society*, "believed in awakening poor people in the cities not only to the franchise but to their own rage."[133] By 1965, some of that rage was bleeding into the playgrounds.

Newark firemen were among the first to feel the heat. As late as the early 1960s, firemen, even in the heart of Newark's Black community, enjoyed good relations with their neighbors. Sitting casually in front of the firehouse, they would often strike up conversations with locals, and the locals felt free to come in and hang out. "An escalation of confrontations with angry citizens had begun around 1965," writes veteran Newark fireman Neal Stoffers in his book on the riots. "By 1967 harassment had become part of the environment."[134] Given the nature of their work, the police inevitably antagonized certain people. The firemen did not. They saved people.

Objectively, the antagonism made little sense. By 1965, ambitious Blacks were beginning to enjoy, if anything, more opportunity than their White neighbors in the military, corporate America, academia, and government. I got a sense of this emerging disparity that spring when I ran into my friend Albert, the kid I recruited to Cub Pack 115. We attended different Catholic high schools, and he didn't play basketball, so our meetings were rare. A year earlier, I had asked him to give me a shout-out on a Sunday afternoon radio show he ran out of his father's popular central city bar, Knobby's. That particular Sunday I would be visiting my uncle Andy and aunt Ellen in their suburban Cedar Grove home. They were impressed by my street cred when "Little Knobby" followed through.

Albert and I got to talking about colleges. I told him about my guidance counselor's response to my college of choice. "Princeton," he laughed. "How are you going to afford that?" Good question. My best strategy was to grow a half foot or so by my senior year and follow Bill Bradley's route to Old Nassau.

When that plan didn't quite work out, I had to go where the money was, and that was someplace with considerably less ivy than Princeton. When I asked Albert about his plans, he said sheepishly, "Columbia."

I was amazed. "Columbia?" I said. "How did you pull that off?"

He was almost too embarrassed to answer. "Oh, it's a Negro thing," he said apologetically. Albert, we both knew, was a good student but not Ivy League good.

The presumed race blindness of the 1964 Civil Rights Act lasted no more than a year, if that. In September 1965, Lyndon Johnson gave the new ethos its official name with executive order 11246. The order entrusted the secretary of labor with the power "to take affirmative action to ensure equal opportunity based on race, color, religion, and national origin."[135]

In urban America, affirmative action would cause unending friction, especially in police and fire departments. This zero-sum game openly pitted working-class Blacks against working-class Whites. Worse, no one was supposed to notice. For the brass to protest affirmative action was to damage their own chances at advancement. For activists to acknowledge affirmative action was to kill the need for their services. The more radical among them had a vested interest in keeping their followers angry and discontented. Progress was anathema to their cause.

The 1960s took its toll on White ethnics in an even more dramatic way. Early in 1965, I went to my first Vietnam funeral. US Army SP4 William Ernest Swaykos, "Rocky" to us, was killed in January. A one-time neighbor and member of my Boy Scout troop, Rocky got that nickname for his swimming ability or lack of the same. To advance in Scouts, he had to swim, and Rocky kept at it until he mastered the art. His persistence was legendary.

Rocky wasn't the only friend to go to Vietnam. Although the myth persists that Blacks were overrepresented among Vietnam casualties, class was a far more accurate mortality gauge than race. For the guys in my neighborhood, college was rarely the first option out of high school. Families did not even think to save for a college fund. Of the dozens of guys with whom I communicated on this project, a solid majority joined the military soon after high school. About half of them ended up in Vietnam.

"I was just too disgusted with changing schools so at the age of sixteen I dropped out and enlisted into the Marine Corps," notes Ben from Barringer. "As I was finishing a two-and-a-half-year tour in Vietnam, the Tet Offensive was starting to kick in and at the same time the Newark riots in the summer of '67 broke out." After what he had seen in Vietnam, Ben was at a loss to understand why certain people "would want to burn down their own neighborhoods."

"You didn't have to be a rocket scientist to know I was going nowhere in Newark," observes Steve, also from Barringer. "The draft was looming, and not many kids from Newark were getting deferred. I decided I wanted to go, but I would decide which branch. I selected the Navy." In the recruitment office, Steve was asked where he wanted to serve. "I said Operation Deep Freeze, or anywhere west coast. So, naturally they sent me to Vietnam. I suppose if you travel far enough west, you will reach Vietnam." Adds Steve, "I have often made jokes that I wanted out of Newark so bad that

I chose Vietnam because it was safer. Even today, I think I was correct."

Dennis, a 1965 Barringer grad, was drafted into the Army and sent to Vietnam as an infantryman assigned to the fabled 101st Airborne Division. Dennis brought one useful skill to the job. Technically inclined, he had built his own ham radio operation as a teen out of the money he saved delivering newspapers. In Vietnam, he found his niche as a MARS—Military Auxiliary Radio System—operator. He went on to make a home-brewed documentary of his experiences in Vietnam.

In December 1965, Tom Hayden went to Vietnam as well, North Vietnam that is. He hoped to assess the "varieties of revolutionary experience"[136] and share that experience with Newark's budding revolutionaries. In the years ahead, he had plenty of opportunity to do just that.

In the summer of 1965, the Highway Department finally came for our house. Although we did not preserve the paperwork, our next-door neighbors, the Hanlons, did. They asked the State for $25,000 for their two-family home, which was considerably grander than ours. The State considered the request "excessive" and offered instead $15,500. If the Hanlons refused this "fair" offer, the State threatened to refer the case to a "condemnation commission." The Hanlons never had a chance. It was time for all of us to leave in any case. The "midnight plumbers" had been stripping the houses of our departed neighbors and setting fires to cover their tracks. At the time, Richie, who lived across Pigs from me, was off in Korea with the US Army. When he came home, there was no home to come home to. His family had moved, and the house was gone.

That summer, my mother, who could be formidable when aroused, had a sit-down with Police Director Dominick Spina. She held Spina responsible for my father's death, and guilt tripped him into to getting us an apartment in Bradley Court, a largely White, relatively safe, low-rise public housing project on the fringe of Vailsburg.

Many years later, my NPD friend Mario and I drove through Bradley Court. Despite the money the NHA poured into it over the years, the project was a wreck. Many of the lower windows had been ripped open. Others were boarded up. Graffiti scarred the buildings. Trash blanketed the withering green spaces. A manned police car sat on the grounds full time. Building design, for projects big or small, was never the primary reason a housing project failed.

Shortly after we moved into Bradley Court, Amiri Baraka moved back to Newark. He had spent the previous decade or so in New York City, sampling just about every variety of leftism then on display in the coffeehouses of Greenwich Village. It was during his "colored bohemian liberal living on the Lower East Side" phase that he wrote his breakout play, *Dutchman*.[137] First staged in March 1964, months after Martin Luther King's "I Have a Dream" speech, *Dutchman* hinted at the nightmare to come. The play climaxes with a White seductress stabbing a defiant Black man to death on a New York City subway—to say the least, not a common occurrence in real life.

The play represents a pivotal moment in the media's relationship with the Black community. As Baraka admits, the reviews were mixed. Some denounced the play as "misogynistic" and others as "full of hatred." That conceded, writes Baraka, "there seemed to me a kind of overwhelming sense from them that something explosive had gone down."[138] Like the seductress in *Dutchman*, the White media were beginning their flirtation with angry Black nationalism. Both the *Herald Tribune* and the *New York Times* offered Baraka writing gigs, and one magazine tried to recruit him to serve as its Deep South civil rights reporter. Going forward, Baraka's fiery brand of Black nationalism would get much better press than was good for anyone other than Baraka.

Two months after Baraka premiered *Dutchman* in New York, Lyndon Johnson previewed his master plan for America in a speech at the University of Michigan. "I intend to establish working groups to prepare a series of conferences and meetings—on the cities, on natural beauty, on the quality of education, and on other emerging challenges," said Johnson in a speech whose grandiosity would have made even FDR squirm. "From these studies, we will begin to set our course toward the Great Society."[139]

Among the more disruptive of Great Society programs was the Office of Economic Opportunity (OEO), run initially by JFK brother-in-law Sargent Shriver. The OEO insisted on "maximum feasible participation" by local community groups in spending the millions of federal dollars the Johnson administration was pouring almost randomly into the cities. The seemingly mindless distribution of government grants alarmed mayors everywhere. "What in the hell are you doing?" Chicago Mayor Richard Daley asked Shriver. "Does the president know he's putting M-O-N-E-Y in the hands of subversives?"[140]

Among the subversives with his hand out was Baraka. Infused with the spirit of Black nationalism and buoyed by the success of *Dutchman*, Baraka abandoned the Village for Harlem. There he found a point of entry into the Great Society through Harlem Youth Opportunities Unlimited (HARYOU). When Baraka first came across HARYOU, the organization was ostensibly trying to set up a program to prevent riots. "What [the program] would be was anybody's guess," writes Baraka of the program, "and we found out when we started coming around there that most of those folks at HARYOU didn't know either."[141] This chaos, times a thousand, was the Great Society.

Exploiting the confusion, Baraka had a Howard University friend submit a proposal for an arts and culture program. To his own surprise, Baraka managed to secure a few hundred thousand dollars for what he calls "Hate-whitey dramas." Participation in these entertainments was restricted to Blacks. Blacks in white face played the White roles. "One evening we sent Shammy with a pistol chasing one of the characters in *Black Ice*," writes Baraka. "The bloods seeing a brother with a gun chasing somebody who looked like a white man made a crowd instantly, and the show began!"[142] To the outside observer, this playacting seemed more like a dress rehearsal for a riot than a way to prevent one. Baraka concedes as much.

"In our naive and subjective way," he notes, "we fully expected the revolution to jump off any minute."[143]

On a visit to New York that summer, Sargent Shriver learned what "maximum feasible participation" looks like at ground level. "When he came with his entourage to the Black Arts building," says Baraka, "we wouldn't let him in. Bad us!"[144] Baraka's sense of mischief and often humorous self-analysis make his autobiography more readable than it might otherwise be. He acknowledges that not all potential funders were keen on his portrayal of White people "as enemies, devils, beasts, etc." Then, too, the money HARYOU raised attracted all manner of hustlers, con artists, even gangsters. Fed up with the infighting and the politics, Baraka retreated to Newark at the end of 1965. He had a rebellion to start.

REBELLION

I read Tom Hayden's book *Rebellion in Newark: Official Violence and Ghetto Response* not long after it came out in 1967. At the time, I thought Hayden's title a romantic way of dressing up what ordinary people in Newark routinely call "the riots." I refer here to Newark's calamitous July 1967 upheaval, the first of its magnitude in the northeast or north central United States. My research, however, leads me to another conclusion: the Munchkins in the streets may have been rioting, but the men behind the curtain were plotting rebellion.

Riot or rebellion, the events of July 1967 were a boon for local moving companies. "Central Avenue around the firehouse was a fairly stable, mostly Irish neighborhood before the riots," remembers one fireman. "That changed after the riots. People were moving out prior to that, but they left in droves after the riots."[145]

Among those orchestrating the mayhem was Hayden. Perhaps to immunize himself from the kind of conspiracy rap that would ensnare him a year later in Chicago—he was one of the Chicago Seven—Hayden takes no responsibility for the "rebellion." In his book, he modestly describes himself as "a white man who has spent the past four years in the Newark ghetto organizing around issues of housing, welfare and political power."[146]

Homegrown civil rights activist Robert Curvin, at the time the head of the local CORE chapter, saw things a little differently. Although allies, Curvin and Hayden were often working at tangents. While Curvin focused on achievable goals, as Curvin puts it, a "piece of the pie for blacks and Puerto Ricans," Hayden and his SDS pals "fancied themselves as potential revolutionaries."[147]

That trajectory put Hayden at odds with the White, heavily Jewish, Clinton Hill Neighborhood Council. The Clinton Hill people, mostly homeowners, were looking for help protecting their neighborhood from the wrecking crews at city hall. Aspiring revolutionaries that they were, the SDS activists let it be known they had no interest in working with people who had "something to protect," that something being their homes.[148]

As Curvin notes, "The SDS organizers scared the hell out of Newark government leaders, especially the police." He believed they spent considerable time "looking forward to a riot." A July 1966 newsletter the SDS crew helped publish ran an article headlined "Seeds of Riot" that warned locals of the violence allegedly being planned by the police.[149] Even the anti-White Baraka blessed "Tom Hayden and his classmates" for their revolutionary fervor. "[They] were around being 'troublemakers,'" he writes approvingly, "which could only add yeast to the whole mixture."[150]

That mixture included, first and foremost, Baraka himself. Once he got his messy personal life together, Baraka bought an old building near downtown Newark and christened it the "Spirit House." If Newark was Casablanca, the Spirit House was Rick's café, the center for the cultural revolution that Baraka hoped to inspire. "It was possible to do work in Newark," he writes. "I was not an exile from New York. I could do work in the city of my birth. And that positive idea began to grow."[151]

Having settled in, Baraka organized the Afro-American Festival of the Arts. Not all the programs proved popular, but one speaker who did make an impact was Howard grad Stokely Carmichael, head of the Student Nonviolent Coordinating Committee (SNCC). Carmichael had recently succeeded in popularizing the slogan "Black Power," a slogan, says Baraka, tha. "lit me up." Adds Baraka, unaware of just how patronizing he sounds, "The festival was my first really organized attempt to bring political ideas and revolutionary culture to the black masses of Newark."[152]

Another Spirit House visitor during this period was Ron Karenga. Karenga had come to Newark to plan the "Second Black Power Conference," the first of which he staged a year earlier in Washington, DC. Like many others, Baraka fell under the sway of "this dynamic little fat man." For eight years, Baraka echoed Karenga in his call for extracting "unchanging" Black values from pre-capitalist Africa.[153] These values served as the foundation for Kwanzaa, a holiday cooked up by Karenga in that same year, 1966.

Baraka also admired the military posturing of Karenga's security forces as well as their emphasis on karate and self-defense. "In my right-around-the-corner version of the revolution," observes Baraka, "I thought that Karenga represented some people who were truly getting ready for the revolution."[154] Not surprisingly, Baraka fails to cite the unchanging Black value that inspired Karenga to kidnap two Black women, strip them naked, and beat them with electrical cords. He was convicted of these crimes five years after birthing Kwanzaa.

Living in the largely Jewish Weequahic section, Cissy Houston, Whitney's mom, sensed the city's unraveling. "And 1967 brought frightening times not just to our family, but to the entire city of Newark, too," Houston writes. "Drugs were spreading everywhere, even creeping into our cozy little village on Wainwright. The city was tense from the rise in crime and frustration with a civil rights movement that was moving a little too slowly and deliberately."

Gung-ho young Newark motorcycle cop Tony Carbo could smell the insurrection in the air. On a warm July evening in 1966, he was assigned to follow a caravan of eight or so cars cruising Newark's Black neighborhoods. Each car held several Black men. At least a few of the cars had loudspeakers. About a dozen Black police officers in unmarked cars followed behind the caravan. "It became very clear to all us police officers assigned to this detail," writes Carbo, "that these scumbags were trying to start a riot by provoking the people in those areas." According to Carbo, the men in the cars were encouraging onlookers to break into liquor stores and "take what's yours." Finally, a Black lieutenant ordered Carbo out of the detail. "You're the only white person here," the lieutenant told him. "If they start anything you're the first one they'll come after." Carbo thanked him and went on his way.[155]

In a curious aside, Carbo points out that one of the ring leaders of the caravan was known to the police at the time but not well known beyond Newark. "Now in this present day and times," writes Carbo, "this pineapple is well known by everyone. This person is not only well known in this country but also in many foreign countries." Carbo's *Memoirs of a Newark, New Jersey Police Officer* was self-published in 2006. Baraka was still alive and well at the time. In his autobiography, Baraka makes no mention of the 1966 caravan. He does, however, talk about riding in a sound truck through the streets of Harlem during the great blackout of November 1965, urging the people on the streets: "Now's the time. They can't see you. Rip these stores off. Take everything."[156] A month after that incident Baraka returned to Newark and added his own personal toxin to an unhealthy stew:

> All these things were in the bubbling. Black Power pressed these issues at a higher level. It pointed out the straight-out apartheid in the South and the neo-apartheid in the North. It raised the issue of black political self-determination and the need for self-sufficiency. The Nation of Islam preached about "doing for self" and how black people were indeed oppressed by the filthy white devil. Black nationalists talked about "the beast" getting big on black people's flesh, and Addonizio and company were living proof of all these nationalist examples. And I'm sure the "left," wherever it was, was also pushing in whatever ways it could.

If Hayden, Baraka, Karenga, Stokely Carmichael, and the Black Muslims were not problem enough, a new and even more radical Black nationalist arrived to join what Curvin calls "an imagined 'revolutionary trajectory.'" This ex-con went by the name "Colonel Hassan Jeru-Ahmed," and he brought with him a cadre of the Blackman's Liberation Army dressed in khaki uniforms. Upon arrival the good colonel zeroed in on the allegedly hottest flashpoint of Black discontent, the clearing of as many as 150 central city acres to build a new, comprehensive medical complex, the future University of Medicine and Dentistry of New Jersey.

Understandably, many raised serious objections to the size of a project that could displace a whole slew of people, including the residents of our old apartment on West Market Street. With my Myrtle Avenue home also scheduled for demolition, I had to wonder, in my vainer moments, where authorities would locate my future presidential boyhood home and library.

Unfortunately for the citizens in the hospital zone, the radicals coming to their defense had less interest in protecting local interests than they did in provoking revolution. For Black nationalists like Hassan, the controversy was pure opportunity. Uninterested in compromise, he had one of his thugs overturn the stenographic machine at a City Planning Board meeting while he tore up the tape. This provocation took place less than two months before the riots broke out. Neither man was arrested. City officials did not want to stir the hornet's nest.

If the media treated Black and Puerto Rican nationalists with something like deference, they openly disrespected gruff, thirty-something Anthony Imperiale, the public face of an emerging White, largely Italian resistance. Cleverer than he seemed, Imperiale knew what the opposition was up to. In the days before the riots erupted, he claimed to have secured documents that showed the long-term planning behind the uprising, not just in Newark but throughout New Jersey. "If Life Magazine takes a picture of a man with a rifle posing," said Imperiale, "it shows that there was a planned riot. It didn't happen by accident. Snipers don't stay by a window because they got nothing else to do."[157] The revolutionary bullshit was about to hit the fan.

THE RIOTS

Here is how the riots started, at least according to *Sopranos* creator David Chase. An Italian gangster compels a Black cab driver to drive the wrong way on a one-way street and to wait for him while he transacts business. After the gangster leaves the cab, two White cops pull up, drag the hapless driver from the cab, and beat him in the street for no apparent reason other than that he was driving the wrong way. Watching this scene, I was dumbfounded. That is *not* how policing worked in 1967 anywhere north of Alabama and probably not even there.

The scene above unfolded in the 2021 *Sopranos* movie, *The Many Saints of Newark*. As a fan of the *Sopranos* show on TV, which only rarely hit a false note, I wondered how Chase could make a movie in which scarcely a note rings true. A September 2021 interview with Chase answered that question. At the time of the riots, Chase "lived out of town—about 20 minutes away by car." A deracinated Italian—the family name was originally DeCesare—Chase grew up as an emotionally unstable only child in North Caldwell, an affluent suburb that even today is only about 1 percent Black. A typical home there might look like Tony Soprano's TV house, which, in fact, is located in North Caldwell. In 1963, Chase graduated from the all-White West Essex High School. Chase's writing partner, Larry Konner, who is Jewish, attended a private high school in Brooklyn.

At the time of the riots, Chase was twenty-one. As he told the friendly interviewer, "Me and my friends would say, 'I hope they burn that place down, those motherf**kers. Corrupt, c**k-sucking white people.'" For the comfortably suburban, the problem was always those other "white people." At twenty-one, Chase could be forgiven his myopic self-hatred. He was likely channeling what he heard on the news or learned in college. At seventy-something, he has no such excuse.

"We had both grown up in that period and had what I guess would be called 'revolutionary consciousness' at that time," said Chase of Konner and himself. "We felt that people needed a refresher course. And it really turned out to be true. There were young, Black people who didn't know anything about the Newark Riots. We just felt that was wrong and people should know about it."[158] Those young Black people would have been better served if Chase had simply told them the truth.

The real-life cabbie at the eye of this maelstrom was as anonymous as his name, John Smith. Like the John Smiths who followed him—Rodney King, Michael Brown, George Floyd—Smith was one of life's losers. He had a revoked driver's license and a string of accidents behind him when the police stopped him for driving the wrong way on a one-way street. Angry with the world, and likely showing off to his female passenger, Smith took out his frustrations on the two Italian cops who stopped him.

When asked for his license and registration, Smith cursed the officers, then opened his door into an officer's chest and punched him in the face. He continued to struggle once the officers got him in the patrol car. So troublesome was Smith they turned the siren on and rushed him to the precinct house. This was not everyday stuff. Once there, Smith refused to leave the car, and a third officer helped carry him into the station. For his part, Smith claimed he could not walk because he had been hit in the groin.

Says the *Report of the National Advisory Commission on Civil Disorders* (Kerner Report), "People saw Smith, who either refused or was unable to walk being dragged out of a police car and into the front door of the station." There is a big difference between unable to walk and unwilling. Experience suggests "unwilling." In his refreshingly unvarnished way, Newark PD Officer Tony Carbo explains routine police conduct circa 1967, "If you hit a cop you most likely got your ass whipped." Short of that, you didn't. Smith likely did take his lumps when the officers put him in his cell. From my own interaction with Newark cops over the years, especially those in my own family, I believe he lied about everything else.

As the Kerner Report acknowledges, most of the criminals in Newark were Black. Crime was accelerating, and Newark's crime rate was among the highest in the nation. That there would be more complaints of police brutality was inevitable. There were so many more arrests and so many more opportunities to resist arrest, especially among the increasing radicalized young. These scenes never look good, and someone often gets hurt: the perp, the cop, or both.

Although Newark statistics are sketchy, in New Jersey robberies and burglaries more than doubled between 1960 and 1967, vehicle thefts nearly tripled, and murders increased more than 60 percent. Newark and the state's other troubled cities—Camden, Paterson, Trenton, Jersey City—were driving those numbers.[159]

According to Police Director John Redden, "Newark reported a higher crime rate from 1960 through 1972 than any other city over a quarter million population." The homicide numbers were most chilling. They increased more than sixfold from 24 in 1950 to 148 in 1972, this despite a shrinking population. "You can talk about different standards of reporting crime," said Redden, "but it's difficult to argue about a body count."[160]

The Kerner Report continues, "Within a few minutes, at least two civil rights leaders received calls from a hysterical woman declaring a cabdriver was being beaten by the police."[161] One of the leaders responding to the scene was Robert Curvin. "Some observers thought he was dead," writes Curvin of Smith. "For everyone on the scene, the anger was intense. One could sense the fury in the air." The death rumor is what sparked the riot. The Kerner Report notes, "As more and more people arrived, the description of the beating purportedly administered to Smith became more and more exaggerated." Indifferent to the facts, professional agitators like Baraka and Hayden lit the fire, and the aimless, angry, increasingly fatherless Black young provided the combustible material. As to those ordinary citizens trapped in the conflagration, no one cared.

Nineteen that summer, I was working on the waterfront staff of a scarily woke, co-ed summer camp for abandoned New York City kids about an hour north of the city. An aspiring young Democrat before the riots started, I was something else afterwards. As I watched the TV coverage of the riots with the other camp staff, urban Blacks and suburban Whites, I knew within minutes that, if push came to shove, we'd be on opposite sides of the barricades. Where they saw "pigs," I saw friends and relatives. Solomon could not have conceived a middle ground.

The Blacks I could understand. The suburban Whites I could not. These were Lenin's "useful idiots" but now with flowers in their hair. As best as I could figure, they were hoping to seek redemption from their Black co-workers by projecting their suburban guilt on to the Whites left behind in the cities. In the years ahead, these people learned nothing. Like Chase and Konner, they continued to filter reality through their "revolutionary consciousness" and imposed their distorted vision on the world. To atone for the sins of their race, more imagined than real, they refused to hold Blacks accountable even to minimal standards of civil behavior. The more dangerous the behavior, the more shrill our guilty friends grew in denouncing anyone, Black or White, who insisted that standards be upheld.

The Whites in Newark, especially the young, saw the world more clearly. Having grown up around and among people of color, they did not romanticize them. They knew them too well to generalize. In my conversations with Newark refugees, I was struck by how many made a point of exempting their Black friends and neighbors from any responsibility for the riots. Unlike their suburban peers, however, they did not exempt the bad guys. As one friend tells me, "I had the guilt beaten out of me a long time ago."

As the rumors of Smith's death spread that Wednesday night, an angry crowd gathered around the Fourth Precinct in the shadow of the massive Hayes Homes. Standing on top of a police car, bullhorn in hand, Robert Curvin tried to prevent violence from erupting. "Before I could dismount the car," writes Curvin, "a hail of rocks and Molotov cocktails rained through the air, aimed at the police and the building right behind me. The burning gasoline slid down the façade of the building."

My late uncle Bob, then a sergeant, was among the police officers defending the Fourth Precinct without benefit of helmets, shotguns, or useful riot gear. Writes a dismayed Curvin, "With nightsticks flailing, the police then charged toward the crowd, and one of the worst riots in American history began."[162] Bob would argue that the riots began a bit earlier, like when the rioters threw Molotov cocktails at the police.

Later that night, firemen came under attack as well. When the crew of Engine 12 pulled in to address a car fire, they were greeted with cries of "get them!" Get them? Firemen? This was less a rebellion than an anti-White pogrom. "When that happened," reported a fireman on the scene, "then bricks and everything started raining from the project which loomed."[163]

The riot was "premature," Anthony Imperiale told an interviewer years later. The rioters "jumped the gun." Once it had begun, however, the agitators wasted little time exploiting it. The first night, Wednesday, July 12, passed without too much damage to property and no lives lost. The second night, July 13, all hell broke loose.

Two sisters with whom I spoke—I'll call them Maria and Rosa—had a front-row seat on the mayhem. The two women, then both adolescents, lived just north of what was Roseville's southernmost main drag, Central Avenue. At the time, Maria thought of her corner of the world as "a nice, friendly neighborhood." Earlier that Thursday, Maria saw something that shook her confidence—Black men carrying long wooden crates into a vacant building on Central Avenue. Later, she saw one man with a rifle on the rooftop.

The sights grew more disturbing. What appeared to be chartered buses were dropping off large groups of Black youths on Central Avenue for no greater purpose than to loot and riot. "No white neighborhoods were attacked," writes Tom Hayden, "though rioting reached the borders of at least four separate white neighborhoods."[164] This neighborhood was one of the four, and the rioting did not reach it spontaneously. The buses remained parked on Central throughout the evening.

Maria calls it "a scene out of a movie you will never forget." Gunshots rang out all over. People were running up and down the street. The girls' mother begged them and their little brother to get away from the windows and lie on the floor of their apartment. "I was scared," says Rosa. "It was like a war zone, and daddy was not there to protect us." With their truck driver father on the road and her mother not knowing how to drive, Maria called her fiancé, John, to come and get them.

As the four of them stood on the sidewalk awaiting John's arrival, the crowds surged up and down Tenth Street, plowing right into them and knocking down the girls' mother. "I do not blame my neighbors," says Maria. "It was all people I had never seen before." A Black neighbor, seeing their distress, offered to take them in, but John came through. He pulled right up on the sidewalk, loaded the family into the car, and hightailed it to the girls' grandmother's house in Iselin, a half hour south on the parkway. The family came back weeks later to pack their belongings, but that was it. Newark was history.

The girls were heartbroken. "I loved Newark," says Maria. "I met my husband on Orange Street in Gruning's. He followed me home. Every teenager played together. We jumped rope together. We played under the streetlights. We used to walk everywhere." The parents borrowed money from family members to buy a crackerbox of a house over the bridge, south of the Raritan. "I can't believe they bought it," says Maria. "Rosa could not wait to get out."

Rosa confirms, "I hated it." Like so many others, she had left her life behind in Roseville, forty-five minutes away on a good day, and on the parkway there are no good days.

That Thursday in July was a good day for Amiri Baraka. Having chosen to drive into the eye of the storm, he gushes about the carnage as ecstatically as a Hitler youth writing about Kristallnacht. "The window breakers would come first. Whash! Glass all over everywhere. Then the getters would get through and get to gettin'," he exults. "Then the fire setters, Vulcan's peepas, would get on it. Crazy sheets of flame would rise behind they thing. Burn it up! Burn it up! Like Marvin had said: Burn, baby, burn!"[165] The sophisticated, anti-Semitic Baraka had to know how his words resonated. As William Helmreich observes, "Jews suffered disproportionately in the riots." He explains, "So many of them owned stores in the affected area."[166]

The more prosaic Hayden watched the action through a Marxist prism. "People voted with their feet," he writes, "to expropriate property to which they felt entitled." He adds, as though he believes what he is writing, "The stores presented what they felt was theirs. Liquor was the most convenient item to steal."[167] In its humble defense, Hayden's Marxist interpretation of events often makes more sense than Kerner's liberal one. "As window smashing continued, liquor stores and taverns were especially hard hit," insists the anonymous writer of the report, presumably with a straight face. "Some of the youths believed that there was an excess concentration of bars in the Negro section, and that these were an unhealthy influence in the community." As my mother might have said, "Yeah, right."

Newark PD's Tony Carbo had an altogether different take on those "youths." Yes, the liquor stores went first, but for no reason beyond the obvious. "Unless you were there with me to see, hear, and feel or to be physically involved in what I saw and went through with my fellow police officers," Carbo writes, "you can't possibly realize how some of us felt, what our emotions were or to visualize what problems and dangers we faced during this rebellious time."[168] The media had little interest in what police officers thought, and academics had even less.

On that Thursday, my uncle Bob was called back to the job and stayed on duty for the next seventy-two hours. Like my mother, his sister, Bob did not go to high school. He went to work as a meat cutter until Uncle Sam called and sent him to Korea. There, in 1953, Bob helped make history by defending Outpost Harry. In one scary week, the Chinese People's Volunteer Army (PVA) launched eighty-eight thousand rounds of artillery at this one critical outpost. A sliver of metal from one of those rounds found Bob's neck and hand. He spent the next several months recuperating in a Japanese hospital. When I asked Bob which experience was scarier, he said, "Newark." In Korea, at least, he knew who the enemy was.

The seventeen-year-old John D. lived about a fifteen-minute walk due south of Maria and Rosa, close to South Orange Avenue. Home alone, he was put on alert by the sound of glass breaking on South Orange Avenue. For safety's sake and to get a better view, he went up to the roof with his dog. "People were running up and down the streets looting. The sirens wouldn't stop," says John. "It was like England during the Blitz." Eventually, he fell asleep on the roof using his dog as a pillow.

The sound of a car horn honking woke him the next morning. John looked down from the roof and saw his boss. John was his ace pretzel vendor, the "king of the pretzel boys."

"Johnny, come down," the boss yelled. "We got to get out." When John saw that his boss's windshield had been busted, he began to understand the urgency. "What you are about to see you will never forget," the boss told him as they drove away. He was right.

"It looked like scene from *War of the Worlds*," says John. "It was horrible. I have tried to force it out of my mind." Just a few years earlier, John had thought of his neighborhood as "the promised land."

By the time John left on Friday morning, the first wave of state police had arrived. They were soon followed by National Guard troops then mustering in the armory a block from my old house on Myrtle Avenue. Democratic Governor Richard Hughes took over control of the situation from Mayor Addonizio and decreed a "hard line." The Newark PD had been shooting over the heads of looters. The rules of engagement were about to change.

For would-be revolutionaries like Hayden and Baraka, this was change for the better. The more bodies that fell in the street, the more recruits they could muster for the war to come. And as with all wars, truth was the first casualty. Not content with the "official score" of twenty-one Blacks killed and two Whites, Baraka imagines "many more blacks killed, their bodies on roofs and in back alleys, spirited away and stuck in secret holes." He adds, "It was no riot, it was a rebellion."[169] No one was killed on Wednesday or Thursday when Newark PD was struggling to control the riot. The rioting began to take its toll on Friday, and the dying continued through Monday.

By pure kismet, one supposes, Ron Karenga's Second Black Power Conference just happened to open in Newark as the riot/rebellion was subsiding. The death count helped Karenga reinforce the conference's theme that "the black struggle in the U.S. was the struggle of a non-self-governing people against genocidal oppressors."[170] It is hard to imagine a less uplifting—or accurate—takeaway message for the Black youth of Newark.

In the years since the riots, beginning with the Kerner Report, there has been endless discussion about whether the rules of engagement were too "hard line," but little attention has been paid to the people of Newark caught in the crossfire, starting with the police and firemen. "But only one policeman and only one fireman were killed," writes the callous Hayden.[171] The word "only," I suspect, provided little comfort to the families of Capt. Michael Moran of the Newark Fire Department and Newark Police Detective Frederick Toto. Between them they left behind ten children. Both were shot by snipers, neither of whom was caught.

Moran was responding to an alarm on Central Avenue. Rather than break down the front door and leave the building open to looters, he threw a ladder up to a second-floor window and was shot as he stood at the base of the ladder. My firemen friends have enormous respect for him. As a captain, under normal circumstances, Moran would have assigned one of his men to make that climb. Given the risk from snipers—they would fire on department vehicles or personnel thirty-three times—he took on the duty himself.

"Controversy still surrounds the source of the bullet,"[172] acknowledges Stoffers, but Moran was standing just two hundred yards from the rooftop where Maria and Rosa saw a Black man with a rifle two days earlier. From his perch across Central Avenue, that sniper would have had an unimpeded view. Whoever the gunmen were, the riot took its toll on

Newark FD. By the time the last embers died out, thirty-five firemen had been injured in the line of duty.

Moran's oldest son, Michael, was fifteen at the time his father died, the same age I was when my father died. "What happened left my family and the city with an emotional scar," said Michael fifty years later. "It's part of my family and part of my life. It's part of who we all are who went through it." Mrs. Moran and her seven children hung on in Newark for another decade before moving to Livingston.[173]

For his part, Hayden was as indifferent to the citizens caught in the middle of the melee as he was to the cops and firemen. "Basic feelings of racial hate were released at white people far less often than was suggested by the media," he writes. "Many missiles were thrown at cars driven by whites but not often with murderous intent."[174] Hayden might have been a good deal less glib if Robert Curvin had not saved his radical White ass from an ironic stomping by the people he had helped radicalize.

Upon hearing about the assault on the Fourth Precinct, Hayden was "eager" to go see the action. So he and Curvin drove toward the precinct. Halfway there, a "rampaging" mob spotted Hayden in the front seat. "There's a white guy here," one of them yelled, and a few members of the mob broke off and came after the car. "We were terrified," writes Curvin. He got out of the car and yelled at the rioters, alerting them that his wife and child were with him. "I am going to turn around and get the hell out of here," he told them. To his good fortune, one humanitarian in the crowd prevailed on the others to let Curvin go.[175]

Whether the intent of the rioters was "murderous" or not, they scared the hell out of anyone, Black or White, who crossed their path. Those victims and near victims started telling their war stories immediately and haven't stopped. Knowing that my Pigs friend Artie was a hunter—they had seen deer hanging from his third-floor porch—the police suggested he turn over his guns lest rioters try to seize them. Wisely, Artie declined their offer.

Phyllis, the Republican mayor, remembers her father and the other men of the neighborhood sitting out on their front stoops, locked and loaded, ready for battle. Carol, the Democratic mayor, remembers her mother having to lie on the floor of the Bloomfield Avenue bus to avoid the shots being fired at it. Lester, home on leave from the Army, also took the "safe" route up Bloomfield Avenue "when a crowd of about hundred from my left front started to throw bottles at the car in front of me." He slammed on his brakes and drove down a side street to get away.

"Our home wasn't in the center of it," writes Cissy Houston, "but we were close enough to smell the smoke, see the flames soaring above the Central Ward, and hear the pop-pop-pop of gunshots. At night we could hear the footsteps of people running along the cobblestone streets, and the gunfire." Houston's instincts varied little from every other responsible parent in Newark. "Our home no longer resembled the safe haven we had envisioned for our children," she adds with regret. "After the riots, John [Houston] and I started thinking about leaving Newark." A lot of people, White and

Black, thought just as she did. And like the Houstons, a lot of them left.

My mother stuck it out. She spent riot week hunkered down in her apartment in the Bradley Court housing project. My brother Bob meanwhile was commuting to his job at the Newark Boys Club via two buses that barely skirted the storm. It amazes him still that they kept the buses running. Aunt Ellen, my former neighbor on Myrtle Avenue, remembers my mother calling her brother Andy and hectoring him, "Your *friends* are burning down the city." Ellen and Uncle Andy participated in a program through their suburban church called "Operation Understanding." That was enough to trigger my mother.

The riot officially ended on Wednesday, one week after it began. Three weeks later, the Italian wife of Newark police officer Joseph Rogan gave birth to a son, also named Joseph. That son would go on to become the world's leading podcaster. At age five, young Joe would join the ethnic exodus from Newark.

The weekend after the riot ended, I returned to Newark and stopped by Artie's for a beer. As we sat out on his third-floor porch—I call it a "deck" in our annual summer game of "who was poorer"—we looked south down the length of Pigtails Alley and ruminated about the week that was. This was the last time I would see Pigs unsevered.

AFTER THE FALL

I n a move that suggests a fair amount of forethought, Tom
Hayden managed to get his book *Rebellion in Newark* published before the year of 1967 was out. In this otherwise
annoying book, Hayden makes one observation that helps
explain not only the riots but also the disintegration of the
city that followed. "Fathers and mothers in the ghetto," he
writes, "often complain that even they cannot understand the
wildness of their kids." They believe, he adds, "that youth is
heading in a radically new, incomprehensible, and frightening
direction."[176]

The Kerner Report makes frequent note of that wildness.
The report authors talk about young people throwing rocks,
starting fires, and breaking windows. This kind of trouble the
authors expected, but some incidents took them by surprise.
"A chicken fluttered out of the shattered window of a poultry
market," they write. "One youth tried to throw gasoline on
it and set it afire." When fire failed to kill the poor bird, a
second youth, six-feet tall, "attempted to stomp the chicken."
In another incident, an adolescent shouted "Black power" at
a sympathetic Black city official, and then he and others proceeded to stone him.

The Kerner authors acknowledge that the profile of the rioters was consistent in all the cities studied. Those who rioted were more likely to have been born in the North than those who did not. They were more likely to prefer the term "Black" to "Negro," more likely to hate White people, more likely to resent successful Blacks, and more likely to express what passed for racial pride, "if not racial superiority."

Having detailed the youthful mayhem, the Kerner Report comes to a conclusion unrooted in any evidence. "What the rioters appeared to be seeking," reads the report, "was fuller participation in the social order and the material benefits enjoyed by the majority of American citizens." If this were not wishful enough, they continue, "Rather than rejecting the American system, they were anxious to obtain a place for themselves in it." This was borderline parody. In Newark, 44 percent of those arrested had a prior police record. If they wanted fuller participation in anything, it was in the spoils of war.[177]

For all the punches pulled, the Kerner authors do not shy from sharing what would prove to be the report's most telling statistic: "Twenty-five and five-tenths percent of the self-reported rioters and 23 percent of the noninvolved were brought up in homes where no adult male lived." More trouble loomed ahead, the authors suggest, as "an estimated 40 percent of Negro children lived in broken homes." I was the same age as the riotous young in 1967. I lived where they lived or at least nearby. But I knew of only one White kid "brought up" in a home without a father, and that kid lived with an uncle. For all the talk of racial disparities, almost no one dared talk about the most critical of them all, the "paternity gap."

"Thinking back to how it was makes me wonder why it all had to change," reflects George Cook on his childhood in Columbus Homes. He knows the answer to his own question: "Increased numbers of welfare dependent families changed the atmosphere." As the riots proved, the offspring of dependent families helped change the atmosphere citywide as well. Although spared the riots—some say the Boiardos saw to that—"the fall-out caused from the perception of the 'riots,'"[178] writes Cook, accelerated flight from his neighborhood.

Even after the riots the city was still burning. Fire consumed twenty-six buildings in the wake of Martin Luther King's assassination in April 1968. Thirty-four buildings were destroyed in a firestorm later that same April. Malicious false alarms were skyrocketing, especially in the public schools. Saboteurs were setting booby traps in buildings before setting fires, hoping to injure or even kill unsuspecting firemen. The radicals' hate-Whitey gospel had found disciples among the young. "The majority of those under forty were still hostile to us," observed one fireman. "We were their enemies." Writes Stoffers, "The fire rate continued to climb, ravishing the Central Ward."[179]

The cultural breakdown that was literally destroying Newark was affecting every major urban center with a substantial Black population. Alabama-born activist Jesse Lee Peterson witnessed the destruction up close, first in Gary, Indiana, then in Los Angeles, where he moved as an eighteen-year-old in 1968.

In LA, Peterson "started learning how to project my anger." The one person who best helped him channel that anger was Louis Farrakhan, last seen back in Newark orchestrating the murder of Malcolm X. The young Peterson knew none of Farrakhan's history, but his message came through clearly. "In Alabama, I had been taught not to hate," writes Peterson in *Antidote*. "In California, my attitude was changing gradually from love to hate. Hate of the white man in particular gave me a satisfying way to explain all my other failures." As Peterson was able to see in retrospect, the message of Farrakhan and others found a receptive audience among the troubled young. "Hate was destroying South Central the way it was destroying Gary."[180]

As Peterson explains, the job market had little to do with South Central's cultural and moral decline. The Southern California economy was booming. Nor was the area riddled with decrepit housing, a common explanation for Black anger in cities like Newark. South Central consisted largely of single-family bungalows built after 1920. "And yet what I saw happening in Gary was happening in Los Angeles," Peterson writes. "Young men were not working. Young women were on welfare. Boys were growing up in homes without fathers. They were taking their anger into the street and finding the family life they craved in their increasingly violent gangs. The commercial heart of South Central was on life support." Even more troubling to Peterson was the violence. More young Black men were dying in the streets of American cities than were dying in the jungles of Vietnam. In Los Angeles, the risk of being murdered increased sixfold from the mid-1950s to 1979.[181]

"At the time, if anything, I was part of the problem," writes Peterson. He worked just enough to keep his car running and the drugs flowing. "The people I partied with were all black," he adds. "They were as rootless and unfocused as I was." If Peterson needed to rationalize his failings, there was always a Farrakhan or Jesse Jackson to remind him who was to blame.

In Newark, the agitators lived right among the youth, none more prominent or proximate than Amiri Baraka and Ron Karenga. The hate they cultivated was spreading like a novel coronavirus. "It got ugly after the riots," says Mac, a Facebook friend from Roseville. His parents, both of Irish descent, bought their home a few blocks from mine in 1958, expecting to stay for the long haul. That wasn't to be. Although the freeway spared their house, just barely, the neighborhood lost its communal strength. "The riots and 280 combined changed the whole dynamic," Mac tells me.

After the riots, local thugs felt empowered. Mac's future mother-in-law was mugged. So, too, was his own mother. As an added incentive to leave, vandals broke into their home and cleaned it out. In the late 1960s, the family packed up and left Newark for good. In the late 1960s, many other Roseville residents made the same decision.

Tommy and his widowed father, an Irish immigrant, decided they, too, had had enough. If the freeway had passed them by, again just barely, the predators did not. Tommy, one of the neighborhood's tough guys, was robbed at knife point and his home plundered. Like many others from Roseville, he reluctantly headed over the bridge and raised his own family some fifty miles south of where he had been raised.

"Interstate 280 had cut through Roseville," writes Moe Berg biographer Nicholas Dawidoff, "and helped its decline from a prosperous neighborhood to a dangerous slum where trash filled the streets and some families gave away their homes as they fled to the suburbs." Berg was not spared the plague that infected his neighborhood. "When anybody saw him in Newark, Berg was always alone," Dawidoff continues. "His fine Black hair had gone gray now. He was thick at the middle, and his skin was creased and sagging. He was an old man and vulnerable to criminals, who mugged him during his walks."[182]

Anchored by their schools and churches, ethnic Catholics did not flee readily. It took John D.'s Quebecois family multiple assaults before they quit their home near South Orange Avenue in 1968. What finally persuaded them to move was the cinder block thrown through his mother's bedroom window. "We were the last ones out," says John, who even then was reluctant to leave the city he loved.

Dependent as they were on public schools, Jews had little choice but to leave. For those like Rabbi Joachim Prinz, Newark's most prominent champion of Black-Jewish cooperation, the departure of his fellow Jews felt like a betrayal of their shared ideals. "Jews had been here for many generations," he said as he stared glumly at the many empty seats in his Clinton Avenue temple. "I felt they belonged here. But I was wrong. It was a European romanticism that was ill-placed."[183]

In his novel *I Married a Communist*, Philip Roth tells the sorry tale of a Jewish couple that stayed too long. "I wasn't going to move out of the city where I had lived and taught all my life just because it was now a poor black city full of problems," Murray Ringold tells narrator Nathan Zuckerman,

Roth's alter ego. "Even after the riots, when Newark emptied out, we stayed on Lehigh Avenue, the only white family that did stay."

The decision proved fatal. "I got mugged twice," Ringold continues. "We should have moved after the first time and we certainly should have moved after the second time." He convinced himself, however, that he could not in good conscience "betray the disadvantaged of Newark." So he hung in until his wife, Doris, was murdered for her handbag. "I realized I'd been had. It's not an idea I like, but I've lived with it inside me ever since," he confesses to Zuckerman. "Doris paid the price for my civic virtue."[184] One wonders whether antiracist scold Tim Wise, who is himself Jewish, would have had the civic virtue to persist as long as Ringold did.

I was blessed with an education that Wise never had, living as I did in the midst of the ultimate urban laboratory. After the Martin Luther King conflagration in April 1968, I did a photo essay of the ruins for a sociology class. In early October 1968, I took our home movie camera to downtown Newark to film a rally in Military Park for George Wallace, the segregationist Alabama governor turned semi-serious presidential candidate.

To get a good perspective, I stood on the low wall surrounding the park. On display before me was a political spectacle the likes of which no other city could have staged. The crowd in front of the speaker's platform, several hundred strong, was heavily male and, I suspect, largely Italian. Behind them in almost equal numbers were protestors, mostly White and young. Many of them held signs along the expected lines of "Sieg Heil" and "Wallace = Racism," but many others held signs reflecting their allegiance to various workers' parties and other radical groups.

Circling the park in a sound truck promoting his campaign for Newark city council was Anthony Imperiale. Instead of fleeing Newark after the riots, Imperiale decided to fight. His resistance did not sit well with everyone. In his otherwise admirable book on Newark's Jewish communities, William Helmreich slams "the vigilante activities of Anthony Imperiale." Helmreich sees Imperiale and his North Ward Citizens' Committee as "a textbook case" of the "violent reactions" that awaited Blacks who moved into Italian areas.[185]

The North Ward residents who saw Imperiale and his crew in action had a different take. He was not resisting Blacks, they argue. He was resisting criminals. "He was a great guy," my old friend Tony tells me. A retired teacher, Tony explains that Imperiale's people often got to crime scenes before the police did. They were particularly attentive to the victims, especially women. "He took care of the North Ward," adds Tony.

Pat, also a former teacher, felt the same. "I had great respect for what Imperiale did for Newark," he says. "He kept it safe and Italian."

When George Wallace took the stage in Newark, the protestors started pushing the Wallace supporters from behind. They lacked the street smarts to know not to mess with a crowd of angry Italians. Just as the conflict was about to combust, the roar of motorcycles distracted everyone. Dismounting from the bikes was the unlikeliest gang of peacemakers Newark had ever seen—the burly, hairy gents from the United Klans of

New Jersey. These fellows inserted themselves between the protestors and the Wallace supporters, facing the protestors, arms crossed in defiance. When the protestors continued to surge forward, a flying squad of the largest cops in Newark entered the park right where I was standing. I wish I still had the film. It was great theater.

In 1968, I was still too young to vote, but my mother cast her ballots for Wallace and Imperiale. I understood why. When Wallace said, "Anarchy prevails today in the streets of the large cities of our country," my mother felt as if he were speaking directly to her. So did many others in Newark. Wallace got 22 percent of the vote in the largely Italian North Ward. In 1968, the defection from the Democratic Party was not limited to Wallace or to Newark. In New York State, a majority of Italians voted for Richard Nixon, the first time that a Republican carried the vote of any of the dominant ethnic groups.[186]

Even moderate Democrats like councilman Steve Adubato felt betrayed by party leaders. "In this community, the minority is us," Adubato told columnist Joseph Kraft. "Law and order is something that really matters. I don't mean racism. I mean being able to send the kids into a Boy Scout troop that can go around the city without a fight. I mean being able to go shopping downtown Newark."[187]

As an ethnic group, Italians had been effectively cleansed from the political landscape. Their resistance was denounced. Their champions were denied status as civil rights leaders. Their protests went all but unheard. "They call me a thug. They call me a Fascist. They call me a racist. They call me a hero," said an exasperated Imperiale in 1969. "Now I can't be all those things."[188] On the plus side, no one accused him of White flight.

Baraka accused him of just about everything else. In his memoir, he introduces his readers to Imperiale as "the Newark racist from the Italian North Ward."[189] For Baraka to call someone else a racist took maximum nerve and/or minimal self-awareness. In his memoir, for instance, he boasts of his response to an earnest White woman who wanted to help his cause du jour. "You can help by dying," he tells her. "You are a cancer. You can help the world's people with your death."[190]

Two days before King's assassination in April 1968, Imperiale had appeared on a news feature produced by NBC's New York City affiliate. In his blunt, seemingly artless way, the plainspoken Korean War vet showed a surprising sophistication in dealing with the media. Rather than attack Baraka directly, Imperiale, a karate instructor, used Baraka's own words against him, even citing the quotation's source. "Let me quote from his speech in the Elizabeth Journal," said Imperiale, "'Rob whitey, rape his daughter, and burn him.'"[191] What shocked Baraka and the media as well is that Imperiale refused to retreat meekly into whiteness. Baraka knew how to intimidate Whites. The Italian subset of that race, he was learning, did not roll over so easily.

In the final analysis, though, it did not matter what Imperiale said or did. The media had chosen sides, and they did not line up with the "Jersey vigilante." The demographics were no friendlier to the Italian cause. The young Black population continued to grow, and the older White population continued to die out or move on, even in North Newark. In 1970, Baraka and his allies succeeded in electing Kenneth Gibson the city's first Black mayor. A few months after the election, the incumbent Gibson beat, Hugh Addonizio, was sentenced to a well-deserved ten years in federal prison on conspiracy and extortion charges. In 1970, I could have beaten Addonizio.

Although he had been instrumental in getting Gibson elected, Baraka quickly lost faith in the new mayor. "We saw everyday how Ken Gibson vacillated, lied, sold himself, and showed his ass to the black community," Baraka writes. And with every one of Gibson's foibles, adds Baraka, "Our views grew more and more loud and caustic."[192]

In 1971, the noise penetrated every household in North Newark. Baraka had managed to line up city, state, and federal funding for a sixteen-story, low-income housing project in this still heavily Italian community. Looking at the conspicuous failure of the nearby Columbus Homes, the locals could not believe that Baraka would persist in this high-rise folly, but persist he did. The media could not believe anyone would dare resist, but there to check Baraka at every turn was Imperiale—in the movie version, James Gandolfini to Baraka's Spike Lee. Other than Brooklyn's Meir Kahane, the founder of the Jewish Defense League, no other White ethnic leader worked as publicly and relentlessly as Imperiale did in defense of what he saw as his peoples' interest.

If nothing else, the Kawaida Towers project showed Baraka's hand. He did not feel the need to even fake an interest in multicultural harmony. "The African name Kawaida was 'threatening,'" scoffs Baraka. Many Italians certainly thought so. Tom, a neighborhood guy, interpreted the project as "a cold slap in the face." The Italian resistance, he tells me, was a way for his *paisanos* "to assert themselves so as to reinforce their identity and honor the memory of previous generations who would have felt betrayed." Imperiale led the resistance or, as Baraka would have it, "mobilized the racist elements of the Italian community against the housing."[193] Having been elected successively to city and state offices, Imperiale eventually prevailed in blocking the project.

The victory was a Pyrrhic one. Despite Imperiale's efforts, North Newark began to erode around the edges. "Eventually the tide of racial unrest was too much for the residents," adds Tom. "Migration to upscale Belleville and Nutley began in earnest. These two towns were long perceived to be for the Italians who 'made it.' Now they became refuges for those who longed for things to be the way they used to be, as delusional as that mindset was."

In 1999, Anthony Imperiale died at age sixty-eight of natural causes. In this regard, he fared better than Meir Kahane, who was assassinated in 1990. Imperiale suffered only character assassination. In the opening sentence of its nuance-free obituary, the *New York Times* described Imperiale as "a race-baiting civic leader and politician from Newark who became a national symbol of the backlash against urban unrest."[194]

By 1999, Baraka's long history of racism, misogyny, anti-Semitism, and homophobia had either been romanticized or forgotten. In August 2002, caught up in the romance,

Democratic Gov. Jim McGreevey appointed Baraka New Jersey state poet laureate. A month later, Baraka rewarded McGreevey by reading his poem, "Somebody Blew Up America," on the first anniversary of 9/11. The money line, "Who told 4,000 Israeli workers at the Twin Towers/ to stay away from home that day," cost Baraka his new gig and clouded the rest of his career. It would have pained Baraka to know that the *Times* used the same key word in the headline of his 2014 obituary as it had in Imperiale's obit fifteen years prior. That word was "polarizing." By 2014, there were no more opposing poles in Newark. If proof were needed, four months after Baraka's death, his son Ras Baraka was elected mayor.

Two years before Baraka's death, Whitney Houston died. Although her parents left Newark for the suburbs in 1970, Whitney could not escape the culture. It caught up with her in a Los Angeles hotel room bathtub where she drowned "due to the effects of atherosclerotic heart disease and cocaine use." In her honor, New Jersey Gov. Chris Christie had statehouse flags flown at half-mast.

Supporters pressured Cissy Houston to stage a memorial service at a downtown arena for her "national treasure" of a daughter. But the deeply Christian Cissy insisted on a funeral for "Nippy" at the New Hope Baptist Church, about a mile from my old home on Myrtle Avenue. "I shared my daughter with the public long enough," said Cissy. "Nippy is coming home!"[195]

LET'M ROW

By the mid-1970s, Bradley Court, the housing project in which my mother and sister were living, had begun its slide into predictable chaos. Stubborn as she was, my mother was not about to leave Newark. She held her nose and moved to the city's last semi-Irish redoubt, Vailsburg, there to live among the people she alone thought of as snobs. What kept Vailsburg intact, even after the riots, was the fact that it was home to most of Newark's police and firemen. When city leaders lifted the residency requirements in the mid-1970s, just about the time my mother moved in, they pulled the plug on Vailsburg.

I arrived in Newark to start my new job on a frigid January night in 1982. I had not been to the city in years. Like many of the dispossessed, when we convened as a family, we convened down the shore. I drove in that first night on streets still ice packed from a storm already two days past. As I wrote in my journal, "Welcome to Newark." I was to stay with my mother on the second floor of a duplex until my wife and daughter joined me in June. For the time being, I had the unheated back bedroom all to myself.

The next morning dawned cold and bright. I walked north on Mead Street toward South Orange Avenue on this brittle

Sunday morning to buy a newspaper. As I headed down the street, I heard a faint voice from the shadows say, "Mister." I turned and saw this little, old Italian lady huddling in a doorway. (Note: Just about all women of grandmotherly age in our world earned the honorarium, "little old.")

"Can I walk with you down to the Avenue?"

"Sure," I said.

She walked slowly, hesitantly. It was not easy to match her pace. She apologized for asking the favor, but her family had moved away as had her friends. She would have, too, if she could have afforded to. She thanked me repeatedly for my humble service.

"After the second mugging," she told me, "I'm afraid to walk by myself."

"I understand," I answered. "I'd be afraid too."

"It's a shame," she said, looking around in dismay.

"What is?" I asked.

"Vailsburg," she sighed. "It ain't what it used to be."

I laughed without intending. The woman didn't understand why. To explain our family's encounter years ago in northern Florida with the haughty Vailsburg lady would have taken too much work. In the two decades since that encounter, Vailsburg had devolved from a place people envied to a place they avoided.

When my friend Barbara moved to Vailsburg in 1964 as a twelve-year-old, she thought her new neighborhood "beautiful." She had been living with her Italian father and her German-born mother in a family compound in the Ironbound section. Once her parents had saved enough money to buy a home, her father, a "Newark loyalist," refused to consider the suburbs. He should have. In the early 1980s, his wife was mugged, and he took to sleeping with a handgun under his pillow. Enough was enough. He soon followed his now married daughters and so many other Newarkers down the shore.

When Barbara's parents moved, Vailsburg wasn't close to bottoming out. By 2022, Mario the cop thought it the most dangerous part of Newark. Our tour of the city convinced me he was right. Roseville fell quicker. In January 1982, on my first day at work, I made a point of driving through the old neighborhood. From my journal:

> Drive through old neighborhood; now trashed. Burnt. One movie [theater] gone (killed two women). Other trashed. Few stores survive. One—Tilman's Stationery, old, traditional, wood floored, familiar—looks ancient, sad…Bodegas etc. Trash shops. Burnt out building.

There are better journal keepers than I, but the impression remains. The neighborhood was shot. If a symbol of its decline were needed, the brick facade of our mainstay movie theater, the Tivoli, had recently collapsed on two women passersby, killing them both. When the weather eased a bit, I visited Myrtle Avenue. Although I-280 cut right through the street, Myrtle was at least bridged. Pigtails Alley was not. The highway I expected. The bars on the windows of the remaining homes took me by surprise. So did the chain link fences and snarling dogs. Up until the time we moved, we didn't even lock our door. No window on the block had bars. All fences were ornamental. The locals dogs had names like "Jingles" and "Freckles."

I found one old friend who had yet to move from his duplex on the north end of the street. A Lithuanian from Pennsylvania coal country, the Bill I knew as a kid was funny, charming, athletic, and uniquely able to talk to us as though we mattered. The Bill I met in 1982 was a grizzled, old alcoholic and a hoarder. His wife had died of early-onset Alzheimer's, and his two children had moved on. He remained, however, as engaging as ever.

Having wandered through the corridors carved out of his floor-to-ceiling newspaper collection, I joined him for a beer in that slice of a dining room not yet swallowed by the clutter. There, he happily regaled me with tales of a neighborhood gone to hell. He was well positioned to tell those tales. With the recent departure of an old Irish couple across the street—I knew the family from my newspaper route—Bill reigned as the block's sole White guy. Apparently, the older couple had been watching TV in their living room when a young gentleman barged in, unplugged the TV, and walked out with it as casually as if he had paid cash. For the couple, that was enough. They were gone within a week.

Bill had his own unique survival strategy. He convinced the neighbors that he was nuts. In Bill's case, that was not much of a stretch. To confirm his derangement, he kept an alligator in the bathtub and would occasionally show it off. In researching this project, I called Bill's son, whom I knew as Billy, a successful wealth manager now living in Tennessee. My first question: Did your father really keep an alligator in the bathtub? Yes, he did. When the alligator hit the three-foot mark, Billy convinced him to get rid of it. The two of them drove the alligator to the Bronx Zoo and dropped it off. Billy, who graduated from Barringer in 1972, did not leave the block until 1977. "It was a tough, scary neighborhood," he told me. "Many houses were empty. You just didn't go out." He had his own share of horror stories, personal and communal.

I had a chance to catch up with Billy when he visited Kansas City about ten years ago. Having inherited his father's natural charm, he made a big hit on both Joan and me. In speaking to Billy I realized how much shared history gets lost when there is no home to go home to. I knew his whole family well. His mother, the block's blonde bombshell, took me for my driver's test and seduced the instructor into letting me pass. His father took us to Yankee games on Ballantine Beer day. His sister spent weeks with us down the shore. Billy knew none of that. At the end of the evening, I pulled out a home movie of Billy's first birthday party that my mother shot. He had never seen it before. Here were his parents, now dead, in their youthful glory and his pretty blonde sister, now lost to schizophrenia, in her unclouded innocence. It was an emotional moment.

In 1982, I also reconnected with my father's cousin, Anna. As kids we spent a lot of time with her family, especially her son Eddie, "Crazy Eddie" to us. Anna had spoiled Eddie to the point of craziness to compensate for the polio death of his much-loved older brother. Polio struck hundreds of thousands of children in that era and messed with the minds of millions of parents.

Never was the difference between Anna's child-raising style and my mother's more clearly on display than the day Eddie, Bob, and I decided to row the mile or two across Barnegat Bay. Without asking anyone, we just took a random rowboat and headed out. At eleven or so, Eddie was the oldest. About ten hours later, exhausted and sunburnt to a crisp, we three struggled back toward the cove where we found the boat. Suddenly, there loomed above us a Coast Guard cutter with my mother at the prow, fuming. When the captain reached over to throw us a line, she grabbed his arm and uttered a phrase so wonderfully apt it deserved to be on her tombstone: "Let'm row."

I knew we were going to pay for this one. Not Eddie. Always quick-thinking, he shouted, "Mom, they kidnapped me." Anna chose to believe him or at least pretended to. Eddie's life skidded sideways from there. The last time I saw him was the night he broke a pool cue over Bob's head on the Point Pleasant boardwalk. That was Eddie enough for my mother.

Anna, now widowed, lived around the corner from my mother. Staying with her was Eddie's nineteen-year-old son, Eddie Jr. Always generous, Anna told my mother I, too, was welcome to live with her when Joan and our daughter Margaret arrived in June. *No way*, I thought, *was my family going to live within rifle shot of this neighborhood*. Like Bill on Myrtle Avenue, Anna had lapsed into an alcoholic haze, her house as much a wreck as her life. I stopped by to say hello, thanked her for the kind offer, and found an excuse to turn it down. For all her failings, no one could accuse Anna of White flight. Again like Bill, she would not leave Newark until they carted her out, which, in fact, they literally did a month or so later.

In the interim, her grandson made a splash of sorts in New Jersey's biggest newspaper. "Youths held in shooting," shouted the *Star-Ledger* headline. When I told the guys at the Housing Authority that one of those youths (pronounced "yutes") was my cousin, my street cred shot up the charts with a bullet. The news, however, was sobering.

> Authorities yesterday announced the arrest of four youths charged with stealing a car in Newark at gunpoint and then using it in the shooting and attempted robbery of a young man in a drive-in movie in Roxbury.[196]

The shooting resonated in Roxbury, a once rural town to which people fled just to avoid Newark-style crime. The victim was in guarded condition. The youths were all from Newark. And only Eddie was named, he being the sole perp over eighteen. Once incarcerated, his first call went to my mother. *This apple*, I thought, *had not fallen far from the tree*.

I was wrong about Eddie. In the age of social media, I was able to reconnect with him and find out what did happen that disturbing night in February 1982. His story speaks to the heart of what went awry in Newark in general and Vailsburg in particular. And as with so many such stories, an indifferent father set the stage for the tragedy to follow.

During his high school years, Eddie had left his mother in New Jersey to live with his father in California. It didn't take. Still in his thirties, Eddie Sr. let his son know the boy was cramping his style. Stung by the rejection, Eddie reluctantly returned to his grandmother's house to finish high school. The year was 1981. Vailsburg High had fallen mightily since

1969 when Brendan from Pigs graduated. By Brendan's estimate, the school was then about 80 percent White, and the education was first class. "Vailsburg," Brendan tells me, "had good teachers for two bad reasons." One reason was that a lot of smart young guys found sanctuary there from the draft. The second reason was that more experienced teachers found sanctuary there from the imploding Weequahic High. If proof were needed of Vailsburg's quality, Brendan's 800 on his Latin SATs makes a compelling case. "I identified more with my experience at Vailsburg than at Harvard," says Brendan.

The Vailsburg High Eddie entered in 1981 was a different school. "I was one of the few white kids," he says offhandedly. Now effectively fatherless and "desperate for friends," Eddie found the wrong ones. Living in his grandmother's garage, he had more freedom than was good for him, and his new running mates took advantage. One day in February 1982 a Black friend gave him a gun. Eddie stored it in one of his late grandfather's gun safes.

The next night, three Black guys, two of whom Eddie had never seen before, showed up at the house asking for the gun. When Eddie refused, the leader of the crew—we'll call him "James"—pulled his own loaded pistol on Eddie and demanded the gun. Eddie complied, but James now insisted Eddie come with him and the others. On foot, James led the crew around the neighborhood until he spotted a middle-age Black man getting into an "old, crappy car." James hijacked it at gunpoint. The adventure was just beginning.

James drove his three companions around aimlessly until they chanced upon the Ledgewood Drive-In Theater in Roxbury. Eddie hoped for a moment he might be able to escape into the crowd, but he never got the chance. After finding a spot and hooking up the speaker, James walked over to a young couple smoking marijuana and asked for their stash. When the young man refused, James shot him in the head.

The three in the car, Eddie included, freaked out. Knowing only Eddie could drive, the other two guys pleaded with him to get the hell out of Dodge. Panicking, Eddie took off with the speaker still attached. The furor caught James's attention who promptly shot at the car to make sure it stopped for him. Eddie spent the rest of the frantic trip back to Newark trying to convince James he had no intention of leaving him behind.

As soon as his new friends dropped Eddie off in Newark, he called the Roxbury Police Department and turned himself in. To prove he was an unwilling accomplice, he volunteered to set up a meeting with the other three. Eddie insisted the police arrest him, too, lest the others think him a "stoolie." The sting worked. The police arrested all four. Fortunately for all of them, their victim survived the shooting.

"I was happy thinking my plan came through," says Eddie, but that plan did not work out exactly as expected. Needing someone to indict, the ambitious Morris County district attorney tried to shift the blame on to Eddie, the only one of the four over eighteen. While the authorities dickered about his fate, Eddie spent eighteen months in Trenton State Prison, more forgotten than condemned. "I was never supposed to be there," he tells me. Now a known snitch, Eddie spent most of that time in protective custody. "I was with the worst of the worst," says Eddie. "I prayed a lot and got closer to God."

How his three companions fared Eddie has no idea. Probably not well. In his book on Columbus Homes George Cook speaks of how intimidating an angry, unmoored kid like James can be. As Eddie's experience attests, one James can pull down his friends. A few can take down a neighborhood.

Fortunately, Eddie had enough good influences on his life, including an attentive aunt and my own mother, to leave prison with his soul intact. In the years since, he has gone on to lead a successful and colorful life, but he has never gotten over the rejection by Eddie Sr. In recounting his adventures, including a remarkable one-on-one meeting with Pope John Paul II in St. Louis, Eddie surprised me by pleading, "But I don't have a father."

"The anger that children feel upon being abandoned is a universal phenomenon," Jesse Lee Peterson reminds us.[197] The one privilege Eddie enjoyed that his Black cohorts did not was the absence of an easy out. He had no one telling him to direct his despair at the White man. No matter how troubled Eddie's childhood, that argument did not fly. Instead, Eddie channeled his anger at abandonment into proving that was he worthy of his father's love.

In 1982, as Eddie struggled with the courts, I struggled to make sense of the Newark Housing Authority. Some random journal entries:

> 2-3: Six tradesmen robbed in one building in one day. 18 murders in one building in one year. Roof contractors only go up and down once a day and then armed.

2-5: Question is whether to shut down high rises. Best decision seems to be no decision. Let them slide.

2-22: Read on page 9 of Newark Star Ledger that fireman was shot on truck while responding to call.

3-5: Question of criminals applying energy. Fellow at Scudder [Homes] who swings from roof into apartments…takes not crown jewels but toasters and what not.

The more I saw of Newark that year the clearer it became that flight was the only rational option for any adult capable of leaving, White or Black. This journal entry from August 16 about a Black man I met through work helps explain why:

Malcolm Ellington, gentleman, unmarried, buys house on Hunterdon Street for 6 or 7 K right after the war. Watches it dwindle to nothing. Unsellable. Unrentable. People breaking in 2 or 3 times a week. Wait for him to take the bus, watch him, then go in.

In between my various strange assignments at the Housing Authority, I continued to look for a place to live when my family joined me in June. My mother suggested I talk to my cousin Micky. "Micky?" I asked incredulously.

"Yes, Micky."

Although Mick was my age, he was my mother's first cousin, the youngest. Like many of the cousins of that generation—my mother and my uncle Bob included—Mick did not go to high school. In fact, he did not get beyond the sixth grade. His parents, both drinkers, were struggling with heath issues and could not move from the eroding Newark neighborhood in which they lived.

My uncle Andy tried to intervene, but Mick was not easily controlled. When I was thirteen Andy recruited me to help. Apparently, Mick had fled the area in a stolen car, and Andy wanted to know where a thirteen-year-old would go. I said, "Florida." Bad guess. They found Mick in Pittsburgh sleeping in the back of a newspaper truck. He had sold the car battery to buy food. When his mother died later that year, he went to the funeral in handcuffs. That was the last I heard about Mick until I returned to Newark in '82. Thus, my surprise.

On meeting with Mick that spring, I learned the rest of his story. Mick's father died a year after his mother. With his older brother in the Army, Mick was on his own. As he tells me, "I liked riding around in cars." The problem was the cars belonged to other people. Not surprisingly, he spent most of his adolescence in institutions, including notorious ones like the New Jersey Training School for Boys, better known simply as "Jamesburg" and long since shuttered.

Once out of the slammer, Mick returned to his old neighborhood and started hanging out with the Doby brothers. Convinced of his good heart, they allowed him to date their sister, the lovely Rose, with her blazing blue eyes. Sure enough, love blossomed on Avon Avenue. In March 1967, months before the riots, my nineteen-year-old cousin married his sweetheart. Given the norms of Irish Catholic America at the time, there was a certain urgency to the affair. That conceded, only those with faith in the American dream could have imagined Mick and Rose's life together would turn out as it did.

To support Rose and his young son, Michael, Mick took whatever job he could get. He did not need a college degree to wield a sledge hammer and dismantle boilers. This he did for as many hours as they let him. He saved his money and, in time, bought his own truck, then a second truck, then his own scrap metal yard, then another truck, and so on and so on. And with Rose handling the paperwork, they bought a shore house, then a second, and so on and so on. Mick and his son Michael, the oldest of three great kids, have moved the family business into environmental remediation, and for them obsolete industrial Newark is a gold mine.

In speaking to Mick, I realized that all the explanations I had read for the fall of Newark—the fall of much of urban America—missed the mark. The family, it seemed clear, was the foundation of any community; the stronger the family, the stronger the community. The most overlooked variable in assessing community strength was the percentage of families headed by a married father. By 1982, that percentage was approaching zero in many Newark neighborhoods.

As Mick understood instinctively, getting married and staying married was indispensable to the success of his family and families like his. In 2020, only 3.5 percent of White married couples and 6.2 percent of Black couples lived below the poverty line.[198] Mick's story was more dramatic than most but not exceptional. Virtually everyone from Newark with whom I communicated on this project did okay in life. Some did better than okay. Most grew up in working-class families, their parents renting the space they lived in. As adults, nearly all own their own homes—a class leap for most.

For males, the path through life took a direction something like this: high school, military, job, marriage, college patched around job and family, home in the (often distant) suburbs. My friend Kenny's path hewed to the norm. Like Mick, Kenny got married at nineteen in 1967 and with similar urgency. He took a variety of jobs to support his young family while attending college part-time until he was old enough to join the Newark Fire Department. After a few years on the job, he and Denise were able to buy a home in Ocean County. Despite a brutal commute of sixty or so miles each way, Kenny spent thirty-eight years with the department, retiring as deputy chief. Today, all four of his children and his eight grandchildren live within a mile or two of their very contented grandparents, close enough to enjoy the backyard pool.

Growing up in Newark, none of us had much of a backyard let alone a backyard pool. None of us ever mowed a lawn. I didn't learn to ride a bicycle until I was thirty. Almost all my friends lived in apartments. Some of their parents did not own a car. No one owned two. No one had a dishwasher. No one had air-conditioning. And mothers dried clothes on clotheslines. When Kenny, Artie, and I play our annual "who was poorest" game, Artie brags about his flat's lack of hot water, Kenny of his family's lack of a washing machine, and I of the boarder living on our second floor. (We don't let Mick play. He'd kill us.)

Admittedly, unlike Artie's and Kenny's, my family did spend a week or two down the shore each summer, but those trips were funded by my parents' poker winnings. The more they won in a given year, the longer we stayed. Like many working-class people in New Jersey, we gambled. I played nickel-dime poker with my parents' friends, chess against the polio-stricken neighbor kid at fifty cents a game, and Scrabble with my mother at a penny a point. So cutthroat were the games that as a fourteen-year-old I spelled out "clitoris" in front of my red-faced mom for the eighty-two points it got me. In reality, none of us was poor. We each had two parents in the home and a mother who put a meal on the table every night.

For those who came of age in Roseville, the phrase "white privilege" evokes a shrug or a snicker. None of our families had accumulated wealth. Our parents had little pull anywhere. As adults in the workplace, our race almost always worked against us. If male, our gender did too. In my case I left academia upon learning that White men in my field were hired only as a last resort. Fortunately, I was married to a female academic. It was her job that took us to Kansas City. Were I gay I would have been doubly screwed.

One privilege that our "whiteness" does afford us is a certain freedom of movement. In large swaths of America, we can forget altogether about race. None of us, I suspect, has ever attended an event or joined an organization prefaced by the word "White." The professional antiracists may not believe this, but in the whitest parts of America, MAGA country included, race is a back-burner issue, if an issue at all. Blacks could visit these same places, move to them if they chose, and be treated well, even fawningly well. Only the persistent hectoring from educators and the media keeps America from accepting African Americans as just another ethnic group. Back in the day, Moynihan recommended a strategy of "benign neglect" toward people of color. This would be a happier country if Washington had listened.

That brings us to the essential privilege, the privilege of agency, a privilege my mother neatly spelled out in her admonition, "let'm row." Let them row. Let them accept the consequences of their actions, and let them learn from that acceptance. This is a privilege any responsible parent of any race can bestow upon a child, but that has become "White" only lately and by default. For the last sixty or so years, progressive elites—activists, educators, journalists, elected officials—have conspired to deny Blacks and other "marginalized" people this privilege. For these elites, observes Shelby Steele, accepting "racial victimization not as an occasional event in one's life but as an ongoing identity" has become, in essence, "the litmus test for being black."[199]

When eight-year-old Dina Matos and her parents arrived in Newark from Portugal in 1975, they enjoyed the privilege of agency in full. Like the Jews and Italians and Irish before them, the Portuguese had no choice but to succeed on their own merits. Not being considered "Hispanic," they came without a pre-established infrastructure of blame and/or benefits.

Upon arrival, Dina settled into her uncle's multifamily house in the weary, polyglot section of Newark known as the Ironbound or, by locals, "down neck." In her memoir, *Silent*

Partner, Dina provides an insider's guide to what life was like down neck for a late-twentieth-century immigrant. "My new neighborhood seemed more like a small town than a large city," writes Matos. "Anyplace I needed to get to—my school, my church, the shops—was not more than a few blocks away."[200] Her father walked to his job at Penn Station, and her mother walked to hers at a grocery store.

Upon arrival, Matos could speak not a word of English. At the local public school, which had a multiethnic mix of students, she learned English well enough that by the sixth grade she was excelling. My friend Tony who taught eighth-grade "shop" down neck during its transitional phase calls the Portuguese an "amazing ethnicity." The two professions they hold in highest esteem, he tells me, are police and teachers.

After one of his Portuguese students misbehaved, Tony recalls, the word got back to the boy's mother even before school was out. This little woman, dressed all in black with her hair in a tight bun "had a right hand Joe Louis would have been proud of." Her son got a taste of it in front of his classmates. He behaved much better after that. Says Tony of the Portuguese, "They saved down neck."

Matos attended the local public high school, East Side, and there joined the history club and the civics club. "What I was really becoming addicted to," she writes, "was America and the idea of being an American in a way that perhaps is impossible to understand for someone who is born here."[201]

After graduating in the top 5 percent of her high school class, Matos, like Philip Roth and Amiri Baraka before her, chose to attend Rutgers Newark. Many of her friends were doing the same or attending the nearby New Jersey Institute of Technology. By this time, too, her family had moved to nearby Elizabeth. The parents were not fleeing anyone. They just wanted a home of their own for their three children. Before the 1950s, this was why most people left the cities behind.

Not too long after Newark's radicals declared the American dream dead, Matos and thousands of other Portuguese brought it back to life. Matos, in fact, would cap a successful career in health care with marriage to an ambitious Irish American on his way to becoming governor. True, Matos had no better luck choosing husbands than her husband, Jim McGreevey, did in choosing poet laureates, but every success story has its wrinkles.

In 1982, I got to experience the Portuguese impact on Newark when I asked a Housing Authority buddy if he knew of a decent place to eat. Workers in our sketchy neighborhood bought most of their meals from food trucks. When he suggested "down neck," I did a double take, but one visit made me a true believer. Walking down the main drag, Ferry Street, I passed any number of lively markets, cafes, bakeries, restaurants, and other retail shops. Although there was more Portuguese spoken than English, I never felt uncomfortable, let alone at risk.

Two particular sights caught my attention. One was a young couple pushing a baby carriage. The other was a brightly lit shop window. Both were signs of a healthy, safe, vital community. At the time, no other commercial corridor in Newark had the same vibe. It reminded me of Roseville circa 1960.

The Ironbound revival put the lie to just about every ortho-dox theory on the city's undoing. During Matos's senior year in high school, Paula Span, writing for the *New York Times*, offered a conventional take on "Newark's Failing Dream" that fully ignored what the Portuguese had accomplished:

> In fact, 40 years ago, Newark hummed with brew-eries, tanneries, shipyards and factories turning out shoes, thread, jewelry, paint, military supplies, radio equipment. But when manufacturing no longer required proximity to its markets, invest-ment capital began to drain out of Newark, leav-ing behind empty factories and stores, unknown quantities of toxic wastes and thousands of unem-ployed workers.

What Span writes may be true, but it is nonetheless irrele-vant. The Ironbound was surrounded by toxic waste sites and empty factories as well as by much of Newark's functioning commerce. The presence of this industry served to keep real estate affordable. The Portuguese exploited the potential of this undervalued area, built a community, and created new jobs. Unlike Puerto Ricans, who arrived in Newark at roughly the same time and in similar numbers, the Portuguese arrived in Newark free from the tentacles of the welfare state. With minimal public assistance, they created a harmonious neigh-borhood for themselves and an attractive destination for out-siders. The Puerto Ricans did not. African Americans have not done so in Newark. Nor have they done so in any city during the civil rights era, and for so talented a group of people, that is a tragedy for the ages.

GOODBYE, COLUMBUS

With its strong families and old world charm, the thriving Portuguese village down neck mirrored Little Italy circa 1950. I never had the chance to visit that neighborhood in its prime, but as a fitting irony perhaps, my last assignment at the NHA was to assess the crumbling monstrosity that replaced it, the Columbus Homes. As usual, I would be escorted by Ben, a large, smart, well-armed Black staffer. "Ben, stand up as they come," reads my journal entry from August 20, "unraveled by thought of Columbus." On August 23, Ben and I began our tour. What follows are some of the things I learned, as recorded in my journal:

> Arrange an apartment for a transfer in morning. Elderly woman moves in in afternoon. Apartment already occupied. NHA won't do anything and squatters have gotten the message.

> [Squatters] rip welded doors off. They go through those. If they can't, they go right through brick walls. Police won't go in building. Firemen get mugged. Shit stolen from trucks.

Brand new lobbies opened up. Within two days vandals had pulled down all the paneled ceilings. Stolen all the aluminum doors. Took them right off the hinges.

Vandals pulled burnt up window frame with truck. Anything goes after dark. Machine guns and rifles stored in building 5.

Old Spanish guy been mugged eight times. Got a gun now. Putting in his own glass because maintenance won't.

Moving in people to apartments without toilet bowls "as is."

33,000 light bulbs in one year.

While we're there, fire is set in vacant building, firemen get mugged.

A week after Ben and I made our tour, HUD honcho James Baugh and his entourage made theirs. In that entourage was a reporter for the *New York Times*. The reporter noted that two of the ten buildings were completely empty. About half of the remaining units were legally occupied, and some two hundred other units were occupied by squatters. The many broken windows and charred remnants of past fires did not do much to inspire confidence.

Baugh was less than pleased by what he saw. "No human should ever have to live that way, no animal should ever have to live that way," he told the *Times*.[202] That said, the solutions

Baugh offered were superficial and sure to fail. He fully over-looked the core problem, namely the collapse of the Black community, due largely to the breakdown of the Black family, unwittingly enabled in each case by well-meaning bureaucrats like himself and encouraged by a complicit media.

In 1994, authorities would level the entire complex much as they had leveled Little Italy forty years prior. The prob-lem, they would tell each other, was building design. "This is the end of an American dream that failed," said Newark Mayor Sharpe James at the demolition ceremony. No, what had failed in Newark was government at all levels.

Given its history and demographics, Newark was collaps-ing faster than other cities, but most cities were cratering at their core, Los Angeles included. For twenty years, Jesse Lee Peterson embodied that collapse. "I was miserable," he writes. "I had no purpose. I even ended up on welfare for a while. I told the authorities I could not work because of my drug use. They gave me a stipend, no questions asked, and put me on food stamps. Thanks! That was just what I needed, depen-dency on top of my anger." That anger led to several ugly racial incidents, in the last of which he spit in the face of a White woman.

That incident finally prompted Peterson to look within. He asked God for clarity, and God provided it. Peterson finally saw that he had been consumed all his life by the anger he felt toward his parents for abandoning him. "It was this hatred," he writes, "that people like Farrakhan and Jesse Jackson fed on. I did not realize it at the time, but Farrakhan, Jackson, and I had something very fundamental in common: our fathers had refused to accept responsibility for us at birth."

Although his father was no longer alive, Peterson realized that to move on he had to forgive his mother. That he did in a memorable reunion. "We embraced, the first time ever without a barrier between us," he writes. "Instantly, God took away my fear and anger and gave me peace." When Peterson let go of his anger toward his mother, he let go of his anger toward White people. Relieved of those burdens, he finally found a purpose in life other than hate and resentment. "I realized now that blacks were not suffering from racism," Peterson continues, "but from denying the real source of their frustration. In denial, they chose to believe the lies they were told about white America."[203]

For perhaps twenty years after this revelation, Peterson got precious little support from the civil rights establishment. Careers had been built and fortunes had been made on the understanding that systemic racism was the cause of virtually all Black misfortune. To these people, Black and White, Peterson was mere irritant.

When Barack Obama emerged as a presidential candidate, Peterson saw a glimmer of hope. Given Obama's embrace of fatherhood, he thought, "Obama might still present a useful example to the many shattered souls within the black community." Obama's Father's Day sermon in June 2008 at the twenty-thousand-member Apostolic Church of God in the South Side of Chicago encouraged Peterson even more.

And with good cause. As the first serious Black presidential candidate Barack Obama was in a unique position to address the problems of the Black family. Once he captured the Democratic nomination in 2008, he revived the themes of the Moynihan report in a strategic move to the center. "Of all the rocks upon which we build our lives, we are reminded today that family is the most important," Obama told the congregation. "And we are called to recognize and honor how critical every father is to that foundation." The reigning civil rights honchos could live with this. They could not live with what followed.

"But if we are honest with ourselves," Obama continued, "we'll admit that what too many fathers also are is missing— missing from too many lives and too many homes. They have abandoned their responsibilities, acting like boys instead of men. And the foundations of our families are weaker because of it."

Obama started chipping away at the very idea of systemic racism as the cause of Black failure. "We know that more than half of all Black children live in single-parent households, a number that has doubled—doubled—since we were children. We know the statistics—that children who grow up without a father are five times more likely to live in poverty and commit crime; nine times more likely to drop out of schools and twenty times more likely to end up in prison."[204]

Everyone knew this, of course, but no one of consequence had dared say so this bluntly in public since Moynihan got spanked. Sure enough, less than three weeks after Father's Day, Obama came in for a spanking of his own. A hot mic at a Fox News studio picked up Jesse Jackson saying to another Black guest, "See, Barack been, um, talking down to Black people on this faith-based—I wanna cut his nuts out." Here Jackson made a cutting motion with his hands and added,

"Barack—he's talking down to black people—telling niggers how to behave."[205] Although the media tried to memory-hole this exchange, Obama got the message. He never raised the issue of fatherlessness again in any meaningful way.

In 2020, with the housing project named in his honor long since razed, city leaders turned their racial animus toward Columbus, the man and icon. The George Floyd mania gave them the excuse they needed to amputate the one symbol dearest to the heart of the Italian community, the epic statue of Christopher Columbus in downtown's Washington Park, a gift nearly a century prior from Newark's Italian community. Without even consulting that community, Mayor Ras Baraka had city work crews rip the statue from its pedestal in the middle of the night.[206]

Baraka claimed the statue's removal was "a statement against the barbarism, enslavement, and oppression that this explorer represents." He then had the moxie to say, "The removal of this statue should not be perceived as an insult to the Italian-American community."

"Insult," no. This crudely symbolic stroke of ethnic cleansing went well beyond "insult." Baraka wasn't through. To quiet the one ethnic community nervy enough to check his father's racist ambitions, he promised that the statue would be kept in storage. This was not a promise he felt obliged to keep. According to my source, the statue "was actually found dumped in an open field next to Route 280."

On a closing note, my police friend Mario made a point of driving me by the pedestal where Columbus once stood. From there, we drove by the bench in front of city hall where a seven-hundred-pound replica of George Floyd now sits. If I might offer a sanitized paraphrase of Mario's thoughts about the icon switch—what f***ing continent did George Floyd discover?

EPIPHANY

On a chill, drizzly day in January 1993, I drove my wife, Joan, and our two daughters, now eight and thirteen, to the homestead of my wife's colleagues at the University College of Galway. Joan had been awarded a Fulbright to teach at the university much as I had been awarded one to teach at the University of Nancy in France ten years prior. Of Irish descent as well, Joan had made Irish studies her area of special interest.

Her friends—we'll call them the "Morans"—had chosen to live a traditional Irish life in rural County Galway. The couple and their three daughters spoke Irish at home and kept house almost as simply and sparely as did their ancestors. I remember gathering in a dimly lit living room that night and watching in wonder as Mr. Moran threw peat into the fireplace. We used peat in our fireplace back in Galway City—everyone did—but we bought ours in brick form at the local gas station. The Moran peat was raw. It looked for all the world like clumps of turf, but it smelled much as ours did, that evocative, acrid scent, the smell of old Ireland.

As Joan and the Morans talked about school, and the girls busied themselves elsewhere, I stared at the fireplace, imagining that my grandfather's grandfather once warmed himself at a peat fire much like this, never suspecting he and his kin would soon be wrenched from their homeland and scattered around the globe. Although not a mystic of any sort, I sensed that I was supposed to be there. I was supposed to be in that very place on that very day, January 6, the Feast of the Epiphany, the day on which, exactly thirty years prior, my father took his life.

Dad died at forty-four. Having just turned forty-five, I had lived to see one more Epiphany than he had, and I was living it in the land we left behind. The suffering of all those who came before me, I realized, my father especially, had allowed me to be here, had allowed me to live a life richer and freer in every conceivable way than even that of an Irish king. The message I took from this oddly mystical moment was simple enough—never forget where you come from.

In May of that year, I took a phone call in the small solarium at the rear of our duplex in Galway City. I remember it being sunny, a rare enough event in an Irish spring. It was my mother. For her to have made a long-distance call *this* distant told me the news had to be grave. It was. The lung cancer had returned. She had months to live. I hesitated a second, searching for words, and then said, "Does this mean I have to let you win at Scrabble?" She laughed. There could be death with dignity after all.

Not until she was dying did my mother leave Newark. It was a good thing. People would have been wary about visiting her had she stayed behind. In nearby Union County during those last days, people did come to visit, friends and family, sometimes solo, sometimes enough for a round or two of poker. Only on the last day did Mom remove the wig and take to her bed.

I stopped by that day and grabbed a few moments alone with her. We both knew it was the end. "Any regrets?" I asked.

"Yeah," she said, "if I had known those damn cigarettes were going to kill me anyway, I wouldn't have given them up five years ago." Dying was not about to make this tough old bird get sentimental. When Freud said the Irish were the only people impervious to psychoanalysis, he had my mother in mind.

I asked if there was anyone she wanted to see before she died. She said yes, Helen Walsh. I had known Helen all my life. She and her husband, Ray, were our neighbors on West Market Street. Her son Raymond was my age and a friend from the beginning. One day, I remember a rummy staggering out of the Carnival Club and asking the age of the two women watching over us. We went over to our moms to find out. Although no more than five at the time, I can still recall the precise answer, twenty-three and twenty-five. In fact, my mother was thirty at the time and Helen at least thirty-five. Helen was Mom's secret sharer.

Helen and Ray left West Market Street soon after we did to be closer to St. Rose. When their block in Roseville failed, they moved to Vailsburg. When Vailsburg failed, they took refuge down the shore. After Ray died, Helen remained alone in Ocean County sixty miles or so from home. To honor my mother's request, I drove down the shore to bring Helen back. By the time we returned, it was too late. My mother died before her old friend got to see her. Such is the fate of the dispossessed. They deserve better, much better—not pity, mind you, not even sympathy, just the truth.

NOTES

1. Sebastian Rotella, "The Writer Behind Sicily's Sly Sleuth," *Los Angeles Times*, February 3, 2009, https://www.latimes.com/archives/la-xpm-2009-feb-03-et-andrea-camilleri3-story.html.

2. "Former First Lady Michelle Obama Speaks at Obama Foundation Summit in Chicago," ABC News, November 1, 2017, YouTube, https://www.youtube.com/watch?v=W1UNGaSlAKQ.

3. "Desperate Haven—The Famine in Dungarvan," Waterford County Museum, https://www.waterfordmuseum.ie/exhibit/web/Display/article/330/4/Desperate_Haven__The_Famine_in_Dungarvan_Despair_And_Death.html.

4. Robin DiAngelo, *White Fragility: Why It's So Hard for White People to Talk About Racism* (Boston: Beacon Press, 2015), 81.

5. Amiri Baraka, *The Autobiography of Leroi Jones* (Chicago: Lawrence Hill Books, 1984), Kindle edition, 7.

6. "Victim Impact Statements," US Department of Justice, https://www.justice.gov/criminal-vns/victim-impact-statements.

7. "Building of a Community: Thanks for the Memories, Roseville," June 17, 1999, https://knowingnewark.npl.org/building-of-a-community-thanks-for-the-memories-roseville/.

8. Elizabeth Bathgate, Hand-Written Roseville History, Newark Public Library Digital Repository, https://archive.org/details/MGNwkWardsandSections010/page/n1/mode/2up.

9. "St. Rose of Lima Church in Roseville (Newark)," Newark's Attic, https://newarksattic.blog/2016/08/12/st-rose-of-lima-church-in-roseville-newark/.

10. Nicholas Dawidoff, *The Catcher Was a Spy: The Mysterious Life of Moe Berg* (New York: Vintage, 1995), Nook edition, 21.

11. David Nasaw, *Children of the City: At Work and at Play* (New York: Anchor Books, 1985), Kindle edition, 145.

12. Ibid., 6.

13. Dawidoff, 28.

14. William B. Helmreich, *The Enduring Community: The Jews of Newark and MetroWest* (New York: Routledge, 1998), 68.

15. Kate Moore, *The Radium Girls: The Dark Story of America's Shining Women* (Naperville: Sourcebooks, 2017), Nook edition, 14. (All references to this story come from Moore's book.)

16. "Put the Kaiser in His Place by Re-naming Newark Streets," City of Newark, https://www.newarknj.gov/news/put-the-kaiser-in-his-place-by-re-naming-newark-streets.

17. Richard Linnett, *In the Godfather Garden: The Long Life and Times of Richie "the Boot" Boiardo* (New Brunswick: Rutgers University Press, 2013), Kindle edition, location 3181.

18. Chrissy Clark, "Analysis: Ibram X. Kendi Raked in Over $300,000 in Speaking Fees," *Daily Wire*, March 16, 2021, https://www.dailywire.com/news/analysis-ibram-x-kendi-raked-in-over-300000-in-speaking-fees.

19. Christina Samuels, "Students Give New Voice to King's Dream," *Washington Post*, January 19, 2000, https://www.washingtonpost.com/archive/local/2000/01/19/students-give-new-voice-to-kings-dream/a14aebaf-ead1-4936-a9d6-c521cdd97132/.

20. Ibram X. Kendi, *Stamped from the Beginning: The Definitive History of Racist Ideas in America* (New York: Bold Type Books, 2016), 358.

21. Baraka, 7.

22. Cissy Houston, *Remembering Whitney: My Story of Love, Loss, and the Night the Music Stopped* (New York: Harper Collins, 2013), Nook edition, 18.

23. Baraka, 3.

24. Houston, 18.

25. Ibid., 19.

26. Ibid.

27. Ibid., 20.

28. Ibid., 36.

29. Ruth Grosman, "Nun Loves Care of 148 Kids Daily," *Newark Star-Ledger*, date unavailable.

30. Jane Jacobs, *The Death and Life of Great American Cities* (New York: Knopf Doubleday, 1961) Kindle edition, 35.

31. Ta-Nehisi Coates, "The Case for Reparations," *The Atlantic*, June 2014, https://www.theatlantic.com/magazine/archive/2014/06/the-case-for-reparations/361631/.

32. Ta-Nehisi Coates, "'This Is How We Lost to the White Man,'" *The Atlantic*, May 2008, https://www.theatlantic.com/magazine/archive/2008/05/-this-is-how-we-lost-to-the-white-man/306774/.

33. Charles Fain Lehman, "What Woke's Worth and Why," *Washington Free Beacon*, June 3, 2021, https://freebeacon.com/culture/what-wokes-worth-and-why/.

34. *Sentinel of Freedom*, May 31, 1881.

35. Erin Blakemore, "The Grisly Story of One of America's Largest Lynching [*sic*]," History, September 1, 2018, https://www.history.com/news/the-grisly-story-of-americas-largest-lynching.

36. Michael Immerso, *Newark's Little Italy: The Vanished First Ward* (New Brunswick: Rutgers University Press, 1997), Kindle edition, location 847.

37. Linnett, location 1235.

38. Michael T. Kaufman, "Peter W. Rodino Dies at 96; Led House Inquiry on Nixon," *New York Times*, May 8, 2005, https://www.nytimes.com/2005/05/08/nyregion/peter-w-rodino-dies-at-96-led-house-inquiry-on-nixon.html.

39. Immerso, location 873.

40. Jack Gould, "TV: Challenge on Racism; James Baldwin Puts Problem Squarely in the Laps of All Americans," *New York Times*, May 30, 1963, https://www.nytimes.com/1963/05/30/archives/tv-challenge-on-racism-james-baldwin-puts-problem-squarely-in-the.html.

41. Charles Zerner, "Big Newark Slum to Be Housing Site," *New York Times*, June 14, 1952, https://timesmachine.nytimes.com/timesmachine/1952/06/14/84324512.html?pageNumber=17.

42. Immerso, location 868–870.

43. Ibid., 866.

44. Special to the *New York Times*, "Mayor of Newark Denies 'Kickbacks,'" *New York Times*, April 12,

1953, https://timesmachine.nytimes.com/timesma-chine/1953/04/12/92698534.html?pageNumber=71.

45. Linnett, location 1146.

46. Steven Malanga, "Why Can't Big-City Democrats Reform the Police?" *City Journal*, June 12, 2020, https://www.city-journal.org/democrats-police-reform.

47. Linnett, location 1326.

48. Immerso, location 875–877.

49. Immerso, location 863.

50. Jerry Izenberg, "Dodgers Great Don Newcombe Saved Himself, Then Saved Many Others," *Star-Ledger*, February 21, 2019, https://www.nj.com/sports/2019/02/dodgers-great-don-newcombe-saved-himself-then-saved-many-others-izenberg.html.

51. Tim Wise," Roadmap to Racial Equity: Allies in Today's World," Charlotte, 2011, Unitarian Universalist Association, https://www.uua.org/ga/past/2011/racial-equality.

52. Barack Obama, *The Audacity of Hope* (New York: Crown, 2006), 330.

53. Tim Wise, *Dear White America: Letter to a New Minority* (San Francisco: City Lights Open Media, 2012), 80–81.

54. Ibid., 19.

55. Anthony Weiss, "For One Day, Newark's Jews Return to Mourn," *Forward*, October 8, 2008, https://forward.com/news/14361/for-one-day-newark-s-jews-return-to-mourn-02655/.

56. Ibid.

57. Eric Rosenthal, "This Was North Lawndale: The Transplantation of a Jewish Community," *Jewish Social*

Studies 22, no. 2 (April, 1960), https://www.jstor.org/stable/4465770?read-now=1&seq=17#page_scan_tab_contents.

58. Ibid.

59. Helmreich, 2.

60. Philip Roth, *The Facts: A Novelist's Autobiography* (New York: Macmillan, 2013), Nook edition, 22.

61. Philip Roth, *American Pastoral* (New York: Houghton Mifflin, 1997), Nook edition, 44.

62. Sherry Ortner, *New Jersey Dreaming* (Durham: Duke University Press, 2003), Kindle edition, 18.

63. Ibid., 83.

64. Ortner, 92–93.

65. Baraka, 24.

66. Colleen O'Dea, "Newark Before the Comeback: A City Marked by White Flight, Poor Policy," *NJ Spotlight News*, September 4, 2019, https://www.njspotlightnews.org/2019/09/19-09-02-newark-before-the-comeback-a-city-marked-by-white-flight-and-poor-policy/.

67. Jacobs, 96.

68. Stefan Novakovic, "The Death of the Highrise: A Brief History of U.S. Public Housing Policy," Skyrise Cities, October 2015, https://skyrisecities.com/news/2015/10/death-highrise-brief-history-us-public-housing-policy.

69. Coates, "The Case for Reparations."

70. George Langston Cook, *The War Zone: A Story of Christopher Columbus Homes Newark New Jersey Projects* (self-pub., 2005), 20.

71. Ibid., 29.

72. Ibid., 32.

73. Lisa Rose, "Joe Piscopo Looks Back on the Origins of the Immortal Jersey Joke, 'What Exit?'" NJ.com, January 20, 2014, https://www.nj.com/super-bowl/2014/01/joe_piscopo_looks_back_on_the_origins_of_the_immortal_jersey_catchphrase_what_exit.html.

74. "East-West Freeway Study: An Analysis of Two Alignments," Newark Public Library Digital Repository, https://archive.org/details/NewarkPlanningBoard025.

75. Tim Hains, "April Ryan to Sec. Buttigieg: How Will Infrastructure Bill Help Deconstruct Racism Built into Roadways?" RealClearPolitics, November 8, 2021, https://www.realclearpolitics.com/video/2021/11/08/april_ryan_to_sec_buttigieg_how_will_infrastructure_bill_help_deconstruct_racism_built_into_roadways.html.

76. Patricia Brennan, "Seven Justices, On Camera," *Washington Post*, October 6, 1996, https://www.washingtonpost.com/wp-srv/national/longterm/supcourt/brennan/brennan1.htm.

77. Natasha Gardner, "The Legacy of Denver's Forced School Busing Era," *5280*, June 2018, https://www.5280.com/2018/05/the-legacy-of-denvers-forced-school-busing-era/.

78. Philip Roth, *Zuckerman Unbound* (New York: Farrar, Straus, and Giroux, 1981) Nook edition, 98.

79. Leah Boustan, "The Culprits Behind White Flight," *New York Times*, May 15, 2017, https://www.nytimes.com/2017/05/15/opinion/white-flight.html.

80. Max Pizarro, "The Irish Make a Last Stand with Carlin against Addonizio in the 1962 Newark Mayor's Race," *Observer*, March 17, 2010, https://observer.

com/2010/03/the-irish-make-a-last-stand-with-carlin-against-addonizio-in-the-1962-newark-mayors-race/.

81. Robert Curvin, *Inside Newark: Decline, Rebellion, and the Search for Transformation* (New Brunswick: Rutgers University Press, 2014), Kindle edition, location 1138.

82. Ibid., location 1289.

83. Leslie Maitland, "Trial Reveals Refusal to Indict Gibson for Tax Fraud," *New York Times*, January 25, 1981, https://www.nytimes.com/1981/01/25/nyregion/trial-reveals-refusal-to-indict-gibson-for-tax-fraud.html.

84. "Excerpts from F.B.I. Transcripts of Tapes Released at the DeCarlo Trial," *New York Times*, January 7, 1970.

85. *The Report by the Select Commission for the Study of Civil Disorder in New Jersey* (Hughes Report), 1967, 28.

86. "Cop Found Dead with Bullet in Head," *Star-Ledger*, January 7, 1963.

87. Carlo Rotella, *The World Is Always Coming to an End* (Chicago: University of Chicago Press, 2019), Kindle edition, 6.

88. Ibid., 68.

89. This and the other material on Michelle Obama is taken from Joel Gilbert, *Michelle Obama: 2024* (Nashville: Post Hill Press, 2022).

90. Rotella, 69.

91. Donda West, *Raising Kanye: Life Lessons from the Mother of a Hip Hop Superstar* (New York: Pocket Books, 2007), 97.

92. Michelle Obama, *Becoming* (New York: Crown, 2018), Kindle edition, 20.

93. "Former First Lady Michelle Obama Speaks at Obama Foundation Summit in Chicago," ABC

News, November 1, 2017, YouTube, https://www. youtube.com/watch?v=W1UNGaSlAKQ&t=2s.

94. Shelby Steele, *A Bound Man: Why We Are Excited about Obama and Why He Can't Win* (New York: Free Press, 2008), 118.

95. Helmreich, 115.

96. Richard J. H. Johnston, "Teachers Beaten in Newark Strike," *New York Times*, February 3, 1971, https://www. nytimes.com/1971/02/03/archives/teachers-beaten-in-newark-strike-group-attacks-15-leaving-meeting.html.

97. Curvin, location 361.

98. Rotella, 190.

99. Helmreich, 43.

100. Philip Roth, *I Married a Communist* (New York: Houghton Mifflin, 1998), Nook edition, 297.

101. "Negro Population Doubled in Newark," *New York Times*, June 27, 1931, https://timesmachine.nytimes.com/timesmachine/1931/06/27/102246785.html?pageNumber=10.

102. James Baldwin, from the film, *I Am Not Your Negro*, 1963, https://catalogofcuriosities.substack.com/p/22-the-white-question.

103. Baraka, 136.

104. Corvin, location 864.

105. Ibid., 852.

106. Ibid., 1397.

107. Ibid., 1458.

108. Ibid., 1834.

109. Alexis de Tocqueville, *L'Ancien Régime et la Révolution (1856)—The Old Regime and the French Revolution, 1856*, in Wendy McElroy, "The Revolution of Rising

Expectations," The Future of Freedom Foundation, May 1, 2016, https://www.fff.org/explore-freedom/article/revolution-rising-expectations/.

110. Baraka, 285.

111. Chris Christie, *Let Me Finish: Trump, the Kushners, Bannon, New Jersey, and the Power of In-Your-Face Politics* (New York: Hachette, 2019), 21.

112. Obama, *Becoming*, 24.

113. Rotella, 135.

114. Cook, 53.

115. Ibid., 56–57.

116. Ibid., 53–54.

117. "Former First Lady Michelle Obama Speaks at Obama Foundation Summit in Chicago," ABC News, November 1, 2017, YouTube, https://www.youtube.com/watch?v=W1UNGaSlAKQ&t=2s.

118. Baraka, 51.

119. Daniel Geary, "The Moynihan Report: An Annotated Edition—A Historian Unpacks *The Negro Family: The Case for National Action* on Its 50th Anniversary," *The Atlantic*, September 14, 2015, https://www.theatlantic.com/politics/archive/2015/09/the-moynihan-report-an-annotated-edition/404632/.

120. Steele, 104.

121. Daniel Geary, *Beyond Civil Rights: The Moynihan Report and Its Legacy* (Philadelphia: University of Pennsylvania Press, 2015), 82.

122. *Hughes Report*, 86.

123. Curvin, location 2725.

124. Jesse Lee Peterson, *The Antidote* (Nashville: WND Books, 2015), Kindle edition, 24.

125. Ibid.

126. Ibid.

127. Roth, *American Pastoral*, 27.

128. Chris Arnade, "White Flight Followed Factory Jobs Out of Gary, Indiana. Black People Didn't Have a Choice," *The Guardian*, March 28, 2017, https://www.theguardian.com/society/2017/mar/28/poverty-racism-gary-indiana-factory-jobs.

129. Paul Sloan, "Gary Takes Over as Murder Capital of U.S.," *Chicago Tribune*, January 2, 1994, https://www.chicagotribune.com/news/ct-xpm-1994-01-03-9401030009-story.html.

130. St. Rose of Lima alumni list, 2008, print copy.

131. Karl Evanzz, "Deadly Crossroads: Farrakhan's Rise and Malcolm X's Fall," *Washington Post*, December 10, 1995, https://www.washingtonpost.com/archive/opinions/1995/12/10/deadly-crossroads-farrakhans-rise-and-malcolm-xs-fall/cc071cca-6239-4c2a-b477-f03cc5c6e0b9/.

132. Amity Shlaes, *The Great Society: A New History* (New York: Harper, 2019), Kindle edition, 73.

133. Shlaes, 82.

134. Neal Stoffers, *A View from the Firehouse: The Newark Riots* (Newark: Springfield and Hunterdon Publishing, 2006), 2.

135. "History of Executive Order 11246," US Department of Labor, https://www.dol.gov/agencies/ofccp/about/executive-order-11246-history.

136. Shlaes, 210.

137. Baraka, 278.

138. Ibid., 276.

139. "President Johnson's Speech at the University of Michigan, The American Presidency Project, https://www.presidency.ucsb.edu/documents/remarks-the-university-michigan.

140. Shlaes, 152.

141. Baraka, 306.

142. Ibid., 307

143. Ibid., 311.

144. Ibid., 310.

145. Stoffers, 34.

146. Tom Hayden, *Rebellion in Newark: Official Violence and Ghetto Response* (New York: Vintage Books, 1967), 4.

147. Curvin, location 1621.

148. Ibid., 1601.

149. Ibid., 1627.

150. Baraka, 364.

151. Ibid., 336.

152. Ibid., 336.

153. Ibid., 336.

154. Ibid., 358.

155. Anthony Carbo, *Memoirs of a Newark, New Jersey Police Officer* (self-pub., 2006), 50.

156. Baraka, 323.

157. "Anthony Imperiale Discusses the 1967 Newark Rebellion," https://vimeo.com/179354946.

158. Brian Tallerico, "It Was What It Was: David Chase on *The Many Saints of Newark*," RogerEbert.com, September 30, 2021, https://www.rogerebert.com/interviews/it-was-what-it-was-david-chase-on-the-many-saints-of-newark.

159. New Jersey Crime Rates 1960–2019, The Disaster Center, https://www.disastercenter.com/crime/njcrimn.htm.

160. "Newark: Extremists Drive Wedge between City Residents," UPI, March 8, 1973.

161. *Report of the National Advisory Commission on Civil Disorders*, https://belonging.berkeley.edu/sites/default/files/kerner_commission_full_report.pdf?file=1&force=1.

162. Curvin, location 113.

163. Stoffers, 6.

164. Hayden, 33.

165. Baraka, 368.

166. Heimreich, 41.

167. Hayden, 32.

168. Carbo, 74.

169. Baraka, 371.

170. Baraka, 375.

171. Hayden, 40.

172. Stoffers, 25.

173. Mark J. Bonamo, "Son of Only Newark Firefighter Killed in 1967 Riots Remembers Tragedy," Tap into Bloomfield, July 13, 2017, https://www.tapinto.net/towns/bloomfield/sections/essex-county-news/articles/son-of-only-newark-firefighter-killed-in-1967-rio-2.

174. Ibid., 33.

175. Curvin, location 1902.

176. Hayden, 17.

177. *Hughes Report*, 131.

178. Cook, 53.

179. Stoffers, 36.

180. Peterson, 28.

181. "Homicide—Los Angeles, 1970–1979," *Morbidity and Mortality Weekly Report*, Centers for Disease Control and Prevention, February 7, 1986, https://www.cdc.gov/mmwr/preview/mmwrhtml/00000841.htm.

182. Dawidoff, 303.

183. Heimreich, 75.

184. Roth, *I Married a Communist*, 298.

185. Ibid., 37.

186. Philip Crass, "The Wallace Phenomenon: The 1968 Presidential Campaign as a Reaction to Change" (thesis, Florida Atlantic University, 1976), http://fau.digital.flvc.org/islandora/object/fau%3A10628.

187. Joseph Kraft, "The Italian Connection," October 2, 1972.

188. United Press International, August 28, 1969.

189. Baraka, 384.

190. Baraka, 285.

191. John Chamberlain, "These Days," *Emporia Gazette*, April 15, 1968, https://newspaperarchive.com/emporia-gazette-apr-15-1968-p-4/.

192. Baraka, 432–433.

193. Baraka, 430.

194. David M. Halbfinger, "Anthony Imperiale, 68, Dies; Polarizing Force in Newark," *New York Times*, December 28, 1999, https://www.nytimes.com/1999/12/28/nyregion/anthony-imperiale-68-dies-polarizing-force-in-newark.html.

195. Houston, 202.

196. Frederick Byrd, "Youths Held in Shooting," *Newark Star-Ledger*, February 28, 1982.

197. Peterson, 88.

198. "Poverty Rate of Black Married-Couple Families in the U.S. from 1990 to 2020," Statista, https://www.statista.com/statistics/205097/percentage-of-poor-black-married-couple-families-in-the-us/.

199. Shelby Steele, *White Guilt: How Blacks and Whites Together Destroyed the Promise of the Civil Rights Era* (New York: Harper Collins, 2007), Nook edition, 67.

200. Dina Matos McGreevey, *Silent Partner: A Memoir of My Marriage* (New York: Hyperion, 2007), 23.

201. Ibid., 29.

202. Alfonso A. Narvaez, "Housing in Newark Appalls a U.S. Aide," *New York Times*, September 3, 1982, https://www.nytimes.com/1982/09/03/nyregion/housing-in-newark-appalls-a-us-aide.html.

203. Peterson, 34.

204. "Obama's Father's Day Remarks," *New York Times*, June 15, 2008, https://www.nytimes.com/2008/06/15/us/politics/15text-obama.html.

205. Jeff Zeleny, "Jesse Jackson Apologizes for Remarks on Obama," *New York Times*, July 10, 2008, https://www.nytimes.com/2008/07/10/us/politics/10jackson.html.

206. "Christopher Columbus: Immortal Genoese," newarkhistory.com, http://www.newarkhistory.com/columbus.html.

ACKNOWLEDGMENTS

I would like to thank the scores of Newark refugees who were willing to share their stories, especially those who went out of their way to help, among them: Maureen Brady, Ken Marcell, Art Warner, Laurita Warner, Roger Wilbert, John Desranleau, Rich Guiliano, Dennis Kane, Tom Walsh, Dan O'Flaherty, Bruce Gaeta, Tony Norcia, my aunt Ellen Hanlon Purcell, my brother Bob Cashill, and an extra shout-out to Frank Santora and my cousin Bob Purcell. Thanks too to my cousin Tom Purcell, the family genealogist, and my agent of long-standing, Alex Hoyt, a Newburgh refugee who believed in this project from the beginning.